The Heart of Reformation Faith

The Heart of
Reformation Faith

THE FUNDAMENTAL AXIOMS
OF EVANGELICAL BELIEF

by Heinrich Bornkamm

TRANSLATED BY JOHN W. DOBERSTEIN

Harper & Row
PUBLISHERS

New York, Evanston & London

This book is a translation of *Das bleibende Recht der Reformation. Grundregeln und Grundfragen evangelischen Glaubens,* copyright by Furche Verlag, Hamburg, 1963. Chapters 6 to 9 are from *Einkehr,* copyright by Vandenhoeck & Ruprecht, Gottingen, 1958.

MS: Theology - 16th century
Protestantism

FIRST EDITION

LIBRARY OF CONGRESS CATALOG NUMBER: 65-15388

C-P

For my sister

MARIELUISE PALM

on her sixtieth birthday

Contents

TRANSLATOR'S NOTE   9

PREFACE   11

I.   Fundamental Axioms of the Evangelical Faith   15

     By Faith Alone . . .
     By Grace Alone . . .
     Christ Alone . . .
     Scripture Alone . . .

II.   Luther's Theology of the Cross   45

III. The Meaning of the Church   56

IV.   The Sum of the Reformation   65

V.   The Abiding Validity of the Reformation   82

VI.   The Reformation View of God   100

VII. The Reformation View of Man   105

VIII. The Reformation View of Life   111

IX.   The Reformation View of Death   117

NOTES   123

INDEX   125

7

Translator's Note

The dialogue that is now going on between the churches, especially the churches of the Reformation and the church of Rome is, happily, spreading beyond conversations between technically trained theologians and official representatives of the churches. Serious laymen on all sides are drawn into the dialogue, and pastors who make no pretension to specialized historical and theological learning are increasingly called upon (and not only when they must prepare a Reformation Day sermon) to give sound and helpful guidance in these hopeful and God-given encounters.

The dialogue of the experts may be based upon documents and statements expressed in more technical form, but this little book by Heinrich Bornkamm, an expert himself and the distinguished professor of church history at Heidelberg University, makes a contribution that can be helpful at every level of conversation. Without a trace of polemics or apologetics he has succeeded in expressing in small compass and simple language what the Protestant as well as the Catholic Christian should know are the fundamental affirmations of the faith of the gospel. The dialogue cannot be a real dialogue except as it honestly faces the issues which both participants sincerely regard as indispensable. Heinrich Bornkamm shows himself to be a profoundly informed, temperate, irenic, yet firm vis-a vis the discussion. This book can be helpful to clergy and laymen on both sides of the divided church; it can serve the common cause.

J. W. D.

Preface

The abiding validity or the enduring truth of the Reformation—is it possible to speak in this way? Can we ascribe unchanging permanence to a historical event in the unceasing flux of history? Dare one do this especially in the history of the church which is moved by the power of the Holy Spirit who makes all things new?

It would in fact be impossible to speak in this way if the Reformation were only a link in the chain of history and if in the Reformation the very source of the church itself, the gospel, had not found fresh expression—true, like everything in the history of the church, in contemporary form and dress, but at the same time with a truth and a power that invade and penetrate every age. The following brief studies attempt primarily to view this truth from three different angles: faith—Christ—the church. We then seek to extract the sum, gauged by the sum of the message of Jesus, and finally to understand its meaning and abiding validity in the light of the historical event of the Reformation—a validity and a never-ceasing question which confront not only the Roman Church, but first of all us Evangelical Christians.

H. B.

11

The Heart of Reformation Faith

I

Fundamental Axioms of the Evangelical Faith

THERE ARE certain fundamental rules and formulations from times past which represent attempts to express the nature of the Evangelical faith. All churches and many religions have such basic canons. But often they seem to us to be like ancient gold coins which have worn out in the course of time and perhaps have completely or almost completely gone out of circulation. And yet when we go looking for new statements of the nature of Evangelical or Catholic or Eastern Orthodox faith, the old gold coins again come to hand and we reach out for them almost automatically. This is reason enough to test them again for their gold content and to ask ourselves whether they do not express something that is determinative and indispensable in our faith, something which we must understand afresh or which we must reappropriate and repossess.

For the Evangelical faith these basic canons are the famous "alone" formulas: by faith alone, by grace alone, Christ alone, the Holy Scriptures alone. And about each of these formulas the question has been asked: Why "alone"? Why so exclusive? It might therefore be a help perhaps if for once we stated these formulas without this negative tone, which is directed against certain misinterpretations, and said: Wholly by faith, wholly by grace, wholly by Christ, wholly by the Scriptures. Put this way the "alone" is not eliminated, and, of course, it cannot be eliminated; but perhaps we would agree that it shifts the tone away from the exclusive word "alone" and puts the emphasis upon the matter itself: faith, grace, Christ, Holy Scriptures. When we better understand the matter itself we will also better understand the word "alone"; but never the other way around.

By Faith Alone

Take one of these fundamental canons of Evangelical faith. In this formula there are two affirmations. One is a statement of how we can know God, namely, through faith alone, not through our thought. And the other is an affirmation of how we can stand before God, namely, only in faith, not through what we do. This is the better known side, the famous question whether we are justified before God through faith or through works or through works and faith. Because this is a traditional question with a long history it is not immediately intelligible to us today. We shall therefore begin with the first signification of these words "by faith alone," which is not thought of as the usual one.

The word "faith" touches the deepest mystery that surrounds us. We live in the midst of a world that speaks to us with a thousand voices, challenging us to reflection. But these voices are at the same time a thousand riddles. Does everything that goes on around us day by day have any meaning, any connection and relationship? When we contemplate the marvelous structure of the plants that emerge from the protecting earth in spring, the lovely colors and the unimaginable variety of the forms of the flowers, the wonderfully subtle and cunning methods by which plants and animals obtain their nourishment, or, for example, the phenomena of symbiosis, the living together of simply structured organisms which provide mutual indispensable help to one another, we can only stand in silent awe before this tremendous intelligence, the inexhaustible ingenuity with which all this has been contrived. We can well understand the men of the Enlightenment who felt an almost rapturous joy in discovery as they saw a fresh proof of God in every new area of nature that was opened up and, in a way that to us today seems pathetic and childlike, constructed an ever new theology from the description of the fishes, the birds, the flowers, and the bees.

But it is not only their enthusiasm that has something pathetic and childlike about it for us today, but also the limitedness of their horizon which prevented them from seeing all that lies behind this wonderful, kindly, and meaningful world. For there is a totally different view: the extravagant wastefulness of nature in which the individual being counts for nothing at all, but only the preservation of the species counts; the cruelties inflicted upon one another not only by human beings but also by animals; the strangely purposeless and absurd mechanisms and phenomena which we often find in nature alongside of all its purposefulness; the frightful catastrophes of flood and drought which can sweep in upon nature and devastate it. Now, does all this argue for God or against him? And we have not yet said anything at all about man, this crown of creation—*and* its prodigy, its discoverer and preserver—*and* its destroyer! Is he, is his radically split nature, his grand and ghastly history, a testimony to his Creator or a proof to be used against him?

Hard questions, over which many have brooded and agonized in vain. But then how can one ever penetrate beyond these thousands of riddling voices? How can one learn something about the God who, according to the Bible and all believers, stands behind this mystery—incomprehensible, but very real? The Evangelical answer is this: in faith, only in faith. And the emphasis here is upon faith, not primarily upon the word "only." The primary thing is the wonder, the miracle, that there should be a link between the incomprehensible, invisible God and me, who seeks after him, who can *only* seek after him, but can never grasp him and his thoughts, this link and connection formed by my believing in him. This is the only bridge between God and me. There are, as it were, no land bridges between God and us, but only the air bridge of faith.

Faith itself is part of the mystery of God. It can no more be forced into existence than one can say anything logically compelling and conclusive about God's existence. Nevertheless it is exactly as real as God is real. It is inherent in the uniqueness of God that he communicates himself to us in this way which cannot be compared with anything else. Faith is something different from every other kind of mental activity that we men can engage in. It cannot be computed as one would compute a result from given facts; it cannot be deduced as one would deduce probable or sure conclusions from certain presuppositions.

But faith is also not poetic fabrication of some other product of the imagination, which lays claim only to a special kind of reality, only a symbolic declarative value. On the contrary, it asserts something altogether real, something all-embracing. It is not merely a partial function of our being, such as an insight of

18

our mind or an expression of a decision of the will. It is rather an expression of our whole being, or—to say it in the most correct way—of our heart. For the heart is indivisible, indefinable; it is our whole self, everything belongs to it. There is such a thing as a prudence of the heart, a discernment of the heart, a feeling, tender or vehement, a love, an imagination of the heart. Here and here alone it dwells. It is our whole self, but our self in a new way.

Faith is an overwhelming and a subduing of the heart for which there are no reasons. Reasons are a matter for discussion. Seen from the point of view of the mind, there are many things that speak in favor of faith and many things that speak against faith. Therefore the decision cannot be made in the mind, the intellect, but only in the heart, in our whole self, which either allows itself to be grasped by the truth of God or not.

No one can say why and how this happens. It is something that grows out of countless and hardly perceptible factors: memories of a childhood security; people whose lives simply gave us a demonstration of faith, or who spoke about it convincingly; words from the holy speech of the Bible; its figures, Abraham, Job, Jesus, who at some time or other took on for us a life and reality which they never had for us before; experiences of life in which our previous faith in men or in ourselves collapsed and that other saving, cleansing possibility, namely, that of faith in God, became true and irresistible.

Who would wish to dissect this mystery? Who would deny it? It is the greatest thing that can happen to a man. For it is not merely an added increment of knowledge or ability. It is rather an increase of life, an addition that always brings with it growing pains and disquietude, but in this way it also brings with it a certainty and security that no thought can give.

Hence there can be no philosophical proofs or reasons for

this faith. To look for them contradicts the very nature of faith. Therefore, according to our Evangelical understanding, we cannot say that God the Creator can be known or even proved with certainty through natural things to be the first cause of everything that exists, as the Catholic Church teaches.[1] According to our view, not only did Immanuel Kant raise irrefutable objections to this but even Luther clearly said that all attempts to cope with the reality of God through our understanding do not even come close to God. And even if, despite Kant, we were able to contrive such a deduction from effect to an ultimate cause, we would not arrive at God, but at most at a kind of technical intelligence, an ordered force, not at the God who fills and transforms our whole heart.

But as has been said, we cannot even conceive of this first cause or motive force, much less God. That a hand from the impenetrable deep rules over my life, that among the thousand riddling voices there is a voice that guides, exhorts, and comforts me, this is something which can only be believed. But this we can do, and this is a thing most wonderful. "By faith alone." The "alone" is the self-evident thing, the ability to believe is the miracle, is, we must say, grace.

If we keep this clearly before us, it will be easier for us to understand the other side of this fundamental Evangelical rule "by faith alone." It means that we can stand before God only in faith, not through our action, through our works. The dust of centuries of theological and confessional controversy lies upon this formulation. We must try to beat it out and understand the words in their simplest sense. Or we may ask, what is really meant by the even more old-fashioned phrase: to be justified by faith? Both mean the same thing. "To be justified" means quite simply: to be just before God. So, how can we be just before God, how can we pass muster before him? Why do we even ask this question? Would it not be enough simply to understand how we can know God, by receiving the knowledge of him into our hearts and not merely into our thinking?

Having said this, however, we have said that knowing God is something different from any other knowledge. He does not demand a part of us but rather the whole man. To believe in God does not mean to be convinced in some unprovable way of his existence, but rather to be grasped by him, to surrender oneself to his transforming power as a whole person. If we are not willing to do this, if we know nothing of him, then we also do not believe in him.

In the whole realm of human thought there is no counterpart to this kind of knowing, We can make this clear in an indirect way only by pointing to that most intimate relationship between persons which is without parallel in human relations, the relation between man and wife. Here too persons learn to know each other more deeply the more they live for and with each other, the more they give themselves to each other. So it is also between God and us, though in an incomparably more sublime way. For two persons have something to give to each other; but we have nothing to give to God but must receive everything from him. The relation between the Creator and his creature is a one-sided relationship. Only in faith can we open our hearts to him. He must fill them and he will fill them. And therefore the more we know of God, the more we become certain of him, the more do we become just before him, the more we become the kind of persons he wants men to be. Only in the faith in which he reveals his secret to us are we transformed into persons who can stand before him. To believe in God and to belong to him are one and the same thing. One is the measure of the other. The more deeply we believe in him, the more we belong to him. The more we belong to him, the more we believe in him.

21

Repeatedly the objection has been made to this fundamental Evangelical rule "by faith alone" that, after all, faith alone is not enough; that surely God also demands that man must do something, that he must perform good works, that he must practice love. And Luther's answer to that was: If that's what you think, you do not know what faith is. Faith is never too little. The truly believing person is the person who is wholly turned toward God. The person who in his heart is overcome by God, with all his conduct, his loving, willing, and giving, belongs wholly to God.

Faith and action definitely belong together. But not as two different things, so that one would have to piece out a faith which is inadequate before God with some special demonstrable works. On the contrary, all the works that a person can possibly do are contained in faith which is complete surrender to God. Faith and love are not two things; rather true faith embraces all the love of which a person is capable. For the source and spring of our love to God and our neighbor lie in faith in God's love. Therefore we cannot stand before God by presenting to him our good deeds, our works of love in the hope and with the petition that he may accept and recognize them. All we can do is to expect from God and pray to God that he will give us all the power for a life that is right and just before him, and we may believe that he will give it to us. This is the meaning of faith and it embraces the whole person. Therefore only in faith can we know anything of God and stand before him.

By Grace Alone

Faith and grace correspond to each other as a cup at the well and the water in the well. The water of grace cannot be obtained and held without the cup of faith; and the cup has meaning and purpose only because of the water which it receives. So grace and faith belong together. Faith is a mysterious, incomprehensible, wonderful overmastering of the heart; it is to be filled with a certainty which cannot be obtained by anything else, whether it be logical reasoning or moral appeals. This certainty is a pure gift. Just as we cannot know God through our thought processes, so we cannot stand before him by our own strength. Both are grace. *Sola fide,* "by faith alone," which Paul and the Reformers taught, is therefore only the other side of *sola gratia,* "by grace alone."

Luther expresses this in the fact that he called his theology a "theology of the cross." In view of what the cross denotes, who could speak of anything else but grace? Here the most dreadful offense of man became a blessing. Nowhere is the thought that we have added or could add anything to this so unthinkable as here. Words like "merit" or "human co-operation" do not cross our lips when we stand at the cross. Here the true situation of man before the face of God is revealed. Words do not suffice to express it. Pictures and music, which touch deeper levels of the soul, can say more about it than works alone; but this grace-message of the cross becomes incomparably moving and true where words and music are met together. And nowhere does this occur more impressively than in Bach's *St. Matthew Passion.*

If we look at the thought content and text of the composition, to which, as we know, Bach himself gave great thought, we see very vividly the role that he assigns to man in the crucifixion story. In the choruses and chorales, which express the faith of the church, and in the arias, in which the individual soul pours out the feelings of the heart, the whole of human experience is summed up as it were in two "double-stops": lament and accusation, and thanksgiving and petition. The first chorus begins with its urgent and fervent call, "Come, ye daughters, help me lament." Then the soul, rapt in profound meditation, contemplates

23

the dreadful event: "Ah, Golgotha! unhappy Golgotha!" But out of this meditation comes not a word of resentment against the wicked world and the offenders who committed this terrible act—as we are so prone to show our indignation over the evils and crimes in the world—but only the accusation which a person must raise against himself. To the question who would betray Jesus, "Lord, is it I?" the chorus replies with utter, undeniable plainness, "'Tis I, I should atone." The answer to that question could hardly be more explicit. Then again comes the question, "Who brought all these pains upon thee? Alas, my sin it was that slew thee! . . ." And after the final verdict upon the behavior of those who were followers of Jesus, at that time, "Then all the disciples left him, and fled," comes nothing else but self-examination, "O man, bewail thy grievous sin."

This is the real situation of the man upon whom God here bestows all his love. He is left with no consciousness of his own accomplishment and value, but only with thanksgiving and petition, which Bach causes to pour forth with overwhelming power:

> To all men Jesus has done well;
> The blind he made to see again;
> The lame he made to walk;
> He spoke to us his Father's word;
> He drove the demons out;
> The sad he set upon their feet;
> The sinners all he did receive.
> These were my Jesus' only faults.

The thankful heart that would give itself to the Lord must pray to him even for the gift of thanksgiving: "I give my heart to thee, O Lord; come thou down and enter there." Everything that moves the heart to be willing to follow him and bear his cross and to pray for his help in doing so always runs out into thanksgiving for an incomprehensible, unmerited gift:

> A thousand thousand thanks to thee for all thy pains,
> That thou didst so esteem my soul's salvation.

Anybody who listens to Bach's *St. Matthew Passion* and understands the one great language of its words and music is hearing the purest, the greatest creation of Evangelical faith in *sola gratia*, in grace alone.

But in our day we still dare not forget that for many people the word "grace" has an alien sound. For them Bach's music, which they would be loath to give up, actually disengages itself from the Word which it means to express. True, for many it may still convey a vague sense of the divine mysteries, but it says no more than that to them. Instead of a message of the grace of God for all men it becomes a testimony of the gift and genius of an artist. This is incomprehensible and wonderful, to be sure, but it is not Bach's message. His message is the message of grace. Between his time and ours a question has arisen that makes the message of grace an almost painful, embarrassing thing: Is it not unworthy of man, this free, responsible being, to be dependent upon grace, to have to pray for grace? There is something very fine about our consciousness of human dignity, and we surely would not wish to disparage it. How much good is done because of it and how much evil is not done when a person says to himself: That is beneath my dignity. This is not false pride, but rather a remembrance of what God intended him to be. And how much more good could be done, how much more evil would remain undone, if every one of us were always really conscious that it is beneath human dignity to tell untruths and half-truths, to hold back the truth because we are cowards or only want to preserve our comfort, to seize unscrupulously upon our own small and great advantages over others, to talk otherwise behind their backs than to their faces, to accept sacrifices and kindnesses as if they were our due without being willing to do the same in similar cases.

The truth is what we have a somewhat contradictory attitude toward our human dignity. We react very sensitively whenever we see it encroached upon. But when it gives us some uncomfortable directions about our own conduct, we suddenly go hard of hearing. We forget that human dignity always means to accept and bear responsibility. Indeed, this is its primary characteristic, not a mere feeling of superiority and dignity. But we have a fatal tendency to forget this decisive mark of human dignity. It is so easy to refuse or limit responsibility, in our personal life and especially in public affairs. To the question of who is the betrayer, "Lord, is it I?" we would all instinctively reply, "Not I," instead of Bach's "'Tis I, I should atone." Why should it be my fault that the priests and scribes persecuted Jesus because of their own narrow-minded beliefs and competitive jealousy, that the people allowed themselves to be worked up into a mass frenzy, that Pilate was a weakling, and that the disciples took craven flight? why should I be held responsible for the fact that the Nazis proclaimed a simplified, violent philosophy that met with very little opposition and set up a reign of terror against which only a few would speak out? And yet there were a few; was I among them? Why should I be responsible for the spirit of our times in which all material values are writ large and enjoyed in comfort, along with all the cheap tricks, large and small, that go with it, the thoughtlessness toward those who have no share in this prosperity, the general lack of spirituality and conscience? Why me?—the question comes quickly to our lips.

But what do we say to that other question that sometimes stirs within us: Did we not go along, did we not keep silent, and do we not do the same thing today? Would we not have done exactly the same thing on Golgotha? Rivalry, weakness, cowardice, mass suggestion, hardheartedness, all these motives which brought Jesus to the cross—are they alien to us? Or to put an even more earnest question: If we attach such great importance to human dignity, where have we laid our whole person and existence on the line for it? And if we have done it once, why not always, whenever we have been challenged?

Human dignity which feels that it is impugned by grace is a tricky thing. It is not so innocuous as we think, but highly charged, and if we make use of it, it can explode in our hands and strike back at us. Our free human dignity, to which we are so ready to appeal, is a beautiful word, but not a truth by which we love. Freedom which accords with human dignity certainly does not mean spending one's life just as one pleases for one's own pleasure and benefit. Rather it means freely to accept the responsibility laid upon us, to be ready and willing to serve, and, if necessary, to deny oneself for the sake of others, for the sake of a great cause. If we take an honest look at ourselves, how much of this freedom have we realized in our lives?

But grace makes us really free. It is a tremendous liberation, as Luther so often attested after his harrowing inner struggle, when a man finally stops looking at himself, at his own moral condition, which is at best merely mediocre, at his own middling good will and the more or less respectable little accumulation of good works or merits, which God in his goodness will not leave unrewarded, or, to put it in modern terms, at the human dignity which he has tried to preserve as best he could in his conduct.

Erasmus, the great humanist and pedagogue, objected to this experience and faith of Luther that man becomes free only through grace. He said that man could not be educated in this way. He declared that the preaching of "grace alone" would become lazy. And if too much emphasis were put upon his bondage to sin, man would become discouraged. We must say to him: Exert yourself, you have the strength to do it and God's grace will help you. But "grace alone," this is a dangerous thing. And down to this day, innumerable people who are serious about the problem of education have echoed what Erasmus said.

But Luther was no less in earnest about the problem of education; indeed, he was even more concerned. Therefore he would not allow the slightest illusion about the real capacity of man. And therefore he appealed, not to the dubious, penultimate human powers, but rather to the sure, ultimate power, to faith in grace. He believed that man at his deepest cannot be educated directly by means of moral demands and coaxing encouragement, but only indirectly, as it were by a mighty detour, by bringing him into touch with God. Only if a man allows himself to be grasped by God's creative, re-creative hand can he be set straight. If one objects to Luther by saying that grace is not enough, that man's own effort must be added to it, he gives the same answer that he gave about faith: Grace is never too little. He who trusts himself to grace and hopes that it will do for him what he could never accomplish himself enters into the sphere of God. And this is more than any education can do. To live with God, really to count on God, is something more, something entirely different from relying on one's own powers. Grace is the never-failing source of renewal. From it streams ever new water into the cup of our faith and into our life, if we do not stop up the channels with our self-justifications, for which we so quickly grasp and which have no standing whatsoever before God.

Grace must therefore become visible in our lives. There is no such thing as invisible grace, any more than there is a faith without love. A faith in grace that has no effect upon us and does not change us would, as Luther once said so well, be only an image in a mirror, a mere appearance and not the true face. So Luther, of all people the great preacher of "grace alone" and "faith alone," kept insisting in his sermons: "Afterwards—that is, after you have learned to believe in God's grace—think of nothing else except doing to your neighbor as Christ has done to you, and let all your works and your whole life be directed to your neighbor. Search out the poor, the sick, and every sort of needy person; help them; let the whole practice of your life consist in being helpful to them, to whoever needs you, as much as you are able, with body, goods, and honor."[2] This is the way Luther describes the life lived by grace.

Christ Alone

Grace is the bridge thrown by God across the abyss that separates us from him. For the one who believes, it is liberation from the past that weighs upon his conscience, but also life for today and for the future. It is a strong jet of fresh water that flows into the cup of a heart that is opened in faith. And the inexhaustible source of this water, says the third basic rule of Evangelical faith, is—Christ alone.

But perhaps here our inner resistance to that word "alone" is even more quickly aroused than in the case of the words "by faith alone" and "by grace alone." Why Christ alone? Is not this an immoderate exaggeration, an injustice, a lack of gratitude to the innumerable other great spirits whom God has given to humanity as helpers and guides? Do we really have to dim their light in order to see nothing but the one light of Christ? Do Plato and Goethe have nothing to say to us for the enrichment of our existence? Did Confucius and Buddha know nothing about God? And if you point to the sufferings and death of Jesus, was not the life of Beethoven also a passion that bore the fruits of self-mastery; and was not the death of Socrates too something very great? Why then this presumptuous exclusiveness: Christ alone?

The young Goethe once gave drastic expression to this protest in a letter to his friend Lavater, accusing him of plucking the feathers of every imaginable bird to adorn his one bird of paradise, Christ. This was, of course, very harsh sarcasm; but when one knows what Goethe's relationship to Lavater was, it was also an expression of his distress that a friend to whom he clung with such great loyalty should make the friendship so difficult by his zealous faith. He knew, naturally, how concerned Lavater was to win him over to what was the most holy thing in his life. Because this was such an honest relationship between two men who wanted the best that each had to offer, perhaps Goethe's satirical comment can help us to make it clear that there was something wrong with this argument between Lavater, the convinced Christian, and the young Goethe, who was at least highly uncertain of his faith. It is a fault that very often creeps into this discussion between those who believe and those who doubt.

"Christ alone"—this does not mean that in order to make Christ unique we have to depreciate every other great spirit. Unfortunately, this is frequently done. We look for other men's weaknesses and search out their limitations in order to show why they are not Christ. But is this really what they wanted to be? And does Christ need the weaknesses of others in order to be what he is? Both as believers and as doubters we too easily allow ourselves to slip into making comparisons and weighing one person against the other, which only leads to a false way of looking at them. And in the case of the Christian this is even worse, for he really ought to know better. He should know that faith does not consist in the conviction that Christ is more than others in this or that respect; but rather that he is something other than all other men. Therefore a false kind of belief almost inevitably acquires an inquisitorial, often actually vicious, way of examining other religious convictions to see how inferior they are and to ferret out the imperfections in the views of other wise spirits—completely contrary to the attitude of the Apostle Paul who said of love: "It does not rejoice at wrong, but rejoices in the right." And if one thinks that he must establish the superiority of Christ by critical comparison with other teachers, this only causes the other person to counter by saying: Much of what Christ said was already expressed in the Old Testament. And we find that similar things were said by Socrates and Plato, and certainly by the wise Chinese philosophers, the founders of religions, by Buddha, and the Hindu mystics. There is so much profundity and genuine piety in the history of mankind which does not stem from Christ, so what is there left that we can say is his alone? And, whatever this is, is it enough to justify setting him apart so exclusively and dismissing the others as nothing at all?

This so often chosen way of understanding the "Christ alone," which faith *must* declare, therefore leads us astray. But it also leads us far away from the New Testament. It was the Apostle Paul, whose statement about love we just quoted, who said, "All things are yours . . . and you are Christ's; and Christ is God's." This is a saying of great freedom, which can show us the way out of this false narrowness and the way to a right understanding of this "Christ alone," on which for Paul everything depended. "All things are yours"—there we are given the whole world. How often Christianity has misunderstood this and set up prohibitions against certain areas of thought or of literature which it rejected as "worldly—" books, manifestations of joy in life such as dancing and the theater, new methods and new discoveries of science! The centuries of wretched rearguard battles to which modern science has delivered church circles are a sad story and they have caused many people all kinds of unnecessary spiritual anguish. Funda-

31

mentally, nothing is forbidden, unless it is base and mean. "All things are yours"—with this one reservation: but "you are Christ's." It is not the world that has limits set upon it, it is rather our hearts that are to be controlled. "Everything is yours"; this means that Plato and Goethe, Mozart and modern art, and even Nietzsche and Karl Marx are yours. See what you can learn from them for the understanding of your neighbor, the world in which you live, and your own self. A mature person who is no longer a child quite rightly resents being forbidden by some external authority to have anything to do with certain intellectual matters. There is, however, an inner standard which we must observe: everything is yours, but you belong to Christ.

What does it mean to belong to someone? There are people to whom we belong with our whole life and who belong to us. They are not discovered by looking for a comparison; they simply exist in a fateful way: parents and children, husband and wife. For a proper marriage is also founded, not upon hardheaded weighing of advantages and disadvantages, but rather upon an irrational event: the fact that I meet this particular person at this time in my life and that love and mutual knowledge grow out of some mysterious depth within us: we belong together. This belonging together always embraces the whole person. It includes the mind as well as the heart, the inner and the outer person. There is nothing that so thoroughly molds and determines our life as the parents from whom we come and our marriage. And we certainly can use these ties to illustrate our relationship to God and to Christ. The Bible does this too. It has no more profound image for God than the image of the father and none more intimate for the fact that Christ and those who believe in him belong together than that of a marriage. To belong to another person means to live through things with that person, through thick and thin, through good days and bad days. It means, if the belonging together is a good one, to live in full, unreserved trust in him.

Naturally, all that is human is only a simile, not the whole reality. When we say "We belong to Christ," this is naturally a completely different relationship from that which we can have to any other person in history. I can love Goethe and gain an infinite amount of wisdom, strength, and comfort from him; but I cannot belong to him with my whole person, I cannot put my whole trust in him, I cannot be sure that in every situation of my life I am safe and secure in him and sustained by him. Goethe, who was so thoroughly aware of his own shortcomings and his limitations, would be horrified if such a thing should be expected of him.

Here is where the "Christ alone" certainly applies, and this means not only the Christ who said something more and something other than others said, but rather the Christ with all that he said and did and is, the whole person of Christ. Faith is a person-to-person relationship, not merely being convinced of certain doctrines and moral precepts. Jesus' words and Jesus' person are inseparable. Both together claim and win the heart, so that we trust ourselves to him and let him lead us. This is a unique relationship and no other relationship can stand on the same level with it. It belongs to a different dimension from our relation to any of the other great spirits of human history whom we gratefully honor.

But—many people may ask—why do we belong to Jesus? What is this other dimension? "All things are yours . . . and you are Christ's; and Christ is God's," says the affirmation of Paul which we quoted. That says something very simple. Even Jesus does not belong to himself, but to another, namely, to God, with body and soul, with his whole being. He is transparent for God. That is to say, we cannot see God, but in the figure of Jesus we see what he is, what his intention and his will are. We cannot hear God, but in every word that Jesus utters we hear the voice of God. His whole person, his whole life and everything he did, are one single, uncompounded reference to God. And faith comes in in order that this may dawn upon a man.

And having said that we can also say that Jesus enters the place where for us God stands, the God who demands the whole of us— through the mouth of Jesus. "You must be perfect, as your heavenly Father is perfect." "Love your enemies, do good to those who hate you, bless those who curse you." "I say to you that everyone who looks at a woman lustfully has already committed adultery with her in his heart." "Blessed are the pure in heart." These are the words of God in the mouth of a man, but *Ecce homo*—what a man is this!

Nobody else can speak to us in this way. We would not allow anyone else to speak to us in this way, because nobody else bears the seal of approval, the perfect suffering for mankind even to death—death on the cross. Because these words come from this mouth, they strike home to every man, and he cannot evade them or parry them by saying, "What about yourself?" They hit home— we need only to look in the mirror of his parables—to the self-righteous pious, the greedy rich man, the everlasting shillyshallier, the man who suddenly goes blind and passes by on the other side when a man lies helpless on the road, the person who whimpers to God and men when he himself is in trouble and is hard as nails when somebody else begs his help. And so we could go on at length; the whole gospel is full of stories about us.

But we hear that same voice telling us about the homecoming of the young man who had squandered his heritage, his good name, and his self-respect and was welcomed without a word of reproach by the father. We hear him saying in the presence of the adulteress, "Let him who is without sin among you be the first to throw

34

a stone at her." We hear him uttering that saying which is simply shocking to all respectability and pious security, "There will be more joy in heaven over one sinner who repents than over ninety-nine righteous persons." And at the end we hear him saying that word that wipes away everything that had been done to him, "Father, forgive them; for they know not what they do." And with both together, the demand that none can escape and the forgiveness from which none is excluded, he enters the place where for us God stands and through his words and through his life he says to us what only God can say to us. And through his words and his life he becomes for us the mouth of God, the image of God, the Word of God in person.

This is the other dimension into which no other man, however great he may be, can enter. We are not detracting from anybody else when we see Jesus confronting us all in this dimension, however important or unimportant we may be. And we can accept and seek to gain fruit from everything that the great spirits of the world bestow upon us. Only when someone says to us that this dimension toward God does not exist or that we do not need Christ in order that it may open up to us, do we have to contradict him and tell him that with all his wisdom he is blind and that he is not seeing something which others, perhaps even we ourselves—though it be only in a groping, fumbling way—have experienced.

It is a wonderful thing when an encounter with Jesus eventuates in this experience. And yet at bottom, if we open our eyes, it is not so difficult. It becomes as inescapable as the disciples once described it: "Lord, to whom shall we go? You have the words of eternal life." And that means at the same time: You are the Living One, not someone in the past. You are the Present One, not someone whom we can only remember, like the other great spirits of

35

history, but one with whom we can live and speak in every time of need and in the daily conversation of the heart. And that is true of none other but Christ alone.

Albert Schweitzer concluded his book, *The Quest of the Historical Jesus,* the work that made him famous as a scholar before he became a missionary doctor, with these words:

"He comes to us as One unknown, without a name, as of old, by the lakeside, he came to those men who knew him not. He speaks to us the same word: 'Follow thou me!' and sets us to the tasks which he has to fulfill for our time. He commands. And to those who obey him, whether they be wise or simple, he will reveal himself in the toils, the conflicts, the sufferings which they shall pass through in his fellowship, and, as an ineffable mystery, they shall learn in their own experience who he is."

Scripture Alone

The last of the four basic rules of the Evangelical faith seems to fall out of line with the rest. We do not mean to set up our thesis, "Scripture alone," as an antithesis to the knowledge of God which may be gained, say, from nature. We said right at the outset that there is no sure knowledge of God or even any proof of the existence of God to be found in nature. We rather interpret the phrase "Scripture alone" in the sense of the question which was raised by the Reformation: Is the Bible a sufficient foundation and transmission of the faith or is some other foundation needed, such as the statements of dogma and other traditions of the church? When we put the question in this way, then we have something different from what we discussed as faith alone, grace alone, and Christ alone. These three concepts have the character of being altogether spiritual, which we may think of as a link with the world of the divine. But "Scripture" sounds human, almost material. The Scriptures are words and letters and thus something that is bound to a specific time. And it crosses our mind that the letter kills, but the Spirit gives life, and after all Scripture itself says this. Does it thereby set aside its own importance? We want, to begin with, only to register the fact that it obviously is at least aware of the problem which we immediately encounter when we hear the words "Scripture alone."

But there are still more problems. All kinds of religions have sacred scriptures in whose absolute truth and superiority to all human wisdom the adherents believe, books from which they take directions for their worship and the rules for living that are pleasing to a god or gods. Judaism has its Torah, its Law, Islam its Koran, Confucianism its "classical and canonical writings," the ancient Indian religion its Veda, its literature of "sacred knowledge." In every case one can observe that gradually a tension arises between the fixed letter of the texts and the ongoing spiritual life and that over the centuries efforts are made to overcome this tension by means of arduous interpretation. And we ask: Is not all this a very human thing, something that is bound to history? How then can we really say that the Bible is a book of divine revelation?

The fact is, of course, that the Bible is a book that comes out of history. But this does not prevent it from being Holy Scripture for us Christians; and we shall speak of this later. But we shall understand it wrongly or fail to understand it altogether if we do not see very clearly that it is a product of history. It is that, because it is "word"—and this always means the "word" of very definite human beings. It is written speech, and speech can only be speech that is uttered in a particular time. The two questions which confronted us are therefore identical. The Bible is letter and yet it is Spirit, it is history and yet eternal truth. This is the point of tension which we must overcome.

In earlier times men thought that this tension could be reduced to zero. They said that spirit and letter, eternity and history, coincide in the Bible. The Spirit is in every letter, the Scriptures are verbally inspired. Since we have learned to think historically we can no longer speak in this way. This view of the Scriptures breaks down, not only because of the numerous scientific and historical errors the Bible contains, but also quite literally because of the letters themselves. Originally only the consonants of the Hebrew words in the Old Testament were written down and not until much later were the vowels added by means of small marks or points. When this was done, many words were wrongly vocalized, given the wrong vowels, and besides, the vowel points are very easily confused with one another. Consequently the text of the Old Testament has at many points been so unreliably transmitted that one has to resort to very uncertain conjectures and emendations of the text, and in not a few passages, despite the infinite pains that have been bestowed upon them, it is quite impossible to say exactly what is meant. In the New Testament too there are a great many variants in the numerous manuscripts and a number of insoluble textual problems.

In a book that has had such a long history of growth this is, of course, not at all surprising. It merely needs to be emphasized over against those who still believe that they can ignore this tension between the temporally determined expression and the timeless truth of the Bible. When this is ignored all understanding ceases. For three centuries now the fact that this tension exists has become more and more clear to us. And fundamentally it makes no difference whether some draw the bow more tightly and others more loosely; in other words, whether some judge more conservatively and others more critically. These are only relative differences.

But far more important than this uncertainty with respect to mere letters is the fact that such a collection of numerous books from widely different epochs must inevitably bear the marks of being bound to the time in which they were written. Legal concepts, political ideas, features of the then prevailing view of nature and the cosmos, customs and forms of social life, must necessarily inhere in the narratives and teachings of the Bible. Much that is recorded was transmitted orally for centuries, and even in the New Testament for decades, before it was written down. Therein lies the possibility of slips of memory and other inaccuracies. Therefore scholarly investigation has had to do its best to subject these accounts to careful examination. The result of this study has by no means been the conclusion that the accounts are wrong, but rather that often they are surprisingly reliable for documents which lie so far back in the past. And here again what matters is not the differences in the individual results. What really matters is that we realize that in the Bible we have the truth of God in a historical, human form. Just as Jesus Christ was not an abstract being, but rather a man in his own country, his own time, his own people, with their own way of viewing the world, so the books of the Bible are expressions that come out of a real history and a very long history. The span of time from the earliest parts of the Old Testament to the latest in the New Testament covers more than a thousand years. It is no wonder that this should result in a great multiplicity of strata. On the contrary, what is amazing is that despite all the changes from the beginning to the end there is such a strong continuity of faith.

But this relation between the human form of Jesus and the human form of the Holy Scriptures will be rightly understood

only if at the same time we see that it defines the content of
the Bible and what it is that makes the Bible Holy Scripture.
And this means that we must define more carefully what the
word "holy" means here. We use the word in very different senses:
time-honored pious customs and practices, certain acts of the
church such as baptism and the Lord's Supper, exalted, holy
emotions that come as we listen to great religious music or look
at an overwhelming landscape. We regard as holy the memory
of a dear person to whom we owe much, a father or a mother.
A wife may have the holy duty of rearing her children in the
spirit of her fallen husband. So we could go on mentioning many
other things to which we apply this extraordinary word. Applied
to the Bible it has a more strict and definite meaning. It is not
simply that for us it is a venerable book which we received from
our forefathers and therefore regard as holy, or that it arouses
holy feelings in us and teaches us holy duties. Rather it is holy
because God speaks in it—not merely in the past but continually.
But if that is so, then it cannot be separated from the living Word
of God, which is constantly speaking to us in the words of men
and the visible figure of Christ. The Bible is therefore not in and
of itself the Holy Scripture, it is not made holy by the sum of
devout and wise thoughts it contains, or by the fruits of faith
which have grown out of it in these thousands of years. This
might only evoke a reverence for it which could still insulate us
from its personal address to us. It is holy because out of this
conglomerate of writings, many-leveled, in part uncertainly transmitted, and bound to their time as they are, Christ comes forth
directly to me, questioning, strengthening, and comforting me.
In the preceding section we attempted to clarify that which is
unique and incomparable in the person of Christ by reference to
Paul's statement that "Christ is God's," and that we belong to
him because he belongs to God. If we remember this we shall

also have a right understanding of what is meant by the word "Holy" in Holy Scripture. It is holy in so far as it belongs to Christ and is determined by him.

Unquestionably there is much in the Bible that is not determined by Christ. The New Testament itself unequivocally declares that "Christ is the end of the law"; the Old Testament understanding of the relationship between God and man has been irrevocably abolished through the coming of Jesus Christ. In the New Testament too there are writings or individual statements concerning which we must ask whether what is said reflects solely the spirit of Christ or whether it still contains an admixture of earlier Jewish thinking. As is well known, Luther said this especially about the Epistle of James (which in certain respects he valued very highly but did not find to be fully in accord with the gospel of Christ) and also about the Revelation of John. One may dispute whether this is correct; but this is not now the point at issue. The question itself, however, is right and necessary; for what the Holy Scripture is becomes apparent only from the vantage point of the gospel, only from the viewpoint of the Word and the Person of Christ and of faith in him. The fundamental Evangelical rule, "Scripture alone," of which we are speaking here, will be rightly understood only if we see in it merely another side of the other rule we spoke of previously, namely, "Christ alone."

The Bible is therefore not a mechanically uniform whole in which every word has equal importance. It is rather something organic, articulated, it has a central meaning from which alone it can be viewed as a whole, and that meaning is Christ and the gospel. Once we understand this the Bible suddenly becomes a wonderful living thing. Then it is no longer a series of books from history that have been strung together; rather everything in it is ordered around this central point and finds its proper place according to its nearness to, or remoteness from, Christ. Much in the Old Testament constitutes only the background from which Christ stands out in shining relief. But there are parts of the Old Testament that already point to him: the praise of God in the Psalms, the strong faith that Abraham or the prophets preserved even in times of complete darkness, the consciousness of the holiness of God and our sinfulness, and the hope that God will come and gather his people despite all the imperfection and unfaithfulness of men. And when a person who keeps firmly in mind the center of the Bible, the gospel of pure grace, he will also acquire an ear for certain differences within the New Testament. When one learns to hear and read the Bible in this way, constantly and unswervingly looking at its center, Christ, then the tension of which we spoke above is released. Then one perceives the Spirit in the letters, the eternal truth in the historical form. The Bible, despite the fact that it is a thing of history, has not passed away because Christ has not passed away, but rather is present and speaks to us and, through that which it has preserved of him, it still today sets us down before the very face of God.

When the Reformers insisted upon the rule, "Scripture alone," they were saying that nothing else can be placed on the same level of this witness to Christ. His words, the accounts of his life, his acts, his suffering and resurrection, and the reflection of all this in the primitive Christian writings is without parallel. It is an inexhaustible wealth in which every age can share anew. Nor can the doctrinal statements in which the church has compressed the content of this New Testament message into brief formulas ever claim the same importance as the message itself.

This was why the Reformers so resolutely set their faces against an ecclesiastical doctrinal tradition which was set up alongside of Holy Scripture, having independent and equal rank with it. Naturally there is a tradition in which the message is handed down from generation to generation. It was through this tradition that we received the Bible, through the fact that it was found to be worth writing down and later to print it, but even more deeply through the fact that it was expounded and made precious and understandable to us by believing men in the church. In every right utterance of its preachers and teachers which comes out of the center of the divine message, the Word of Christ lives on. This is an unbreakable continuity.

In this passing on of the tradition new thoughts and new formulations arise; for, after all, the transmission of a truth does not mean literal recitation but rather appropriation of it. And we can appropriate and make it our own only by assimilating it into our own thought and language. But then the original and what is transmitted is always derived and is subject to change. And precisely therein lies its value and also the freedom it gives to us. In the transmission the gospel can and must be set forth and expounded in the way in which a particular age can understand and use it. In this process, formulations may be found which express something that remains valid over long periods of time. But as time goes on it almost always happens that the exposition itself must be re-expounded. And this too may make good sense. But when this is done it becomes even more necessary to search for new thoughts and new words in the living communication of the divine message in order that we may appropriate it. Then the old formulations must give way; they have performed their service. A church which canonizes forever its own traditions puts on an armor that grows heavier and heavier. But Christ, his gospel, and the reflection of it in the faith of those who have gathered about him and taken the step which is determinative of all the future, the step of building his church—this is the bedrock on which the church rests. And ever anew, this fundamental rule of Evangelical faith, "Scripture alone," points the way to this bedrock of the church.

This fourfold "alone"—faith alone, grace alone, Christ alone, Scripture alone—sounds exclusive and repellent. But this is true only of false views of it. In a deeper sense its intent is to extend an invitation, to offer a gift, which we can only pass on to others: a life lived wholly by faith, wholly by grace, wholly by Christ, and wholly by the Holy Scriptures. It is a life lived in a freedom and a fullness that needs no supplementation.

II

Luther's Theology of the Cross

THE CROSS of Christ binds together the whole of Christendom; it stands on the altars of all confessions. Every Christian who is burdened by the cross of his sin and his suffering looks with trust and adoration to the Crucified. If Christendom is at one in anything, it is in the singing of "O sacred Head, now wounded," *"Salve caput cruentatum."*

What point can there be, then, in speaking of Luther's theology of the cross in particular and seeing in it an expression of the essence of his particular proclamation? This is what is being done in modern Evangelical theology. In doing so it is merely adopting a term which was used by Luther and especially frequently in the early years of the Reformation when he was obliged to search most carefully for terms which expressed what was peculiar, distinctive, and different in his theology over against the thinking of his time.

So it is always in the great fundamental questions that stand between the confessions; the differences always lie in what is held in common. And if we want to comprehend the understanding of faith held by the various Christian confessions, we cannot avoid disclosing the differences even in that which is undoubtedly over common possession. But quite as seriously we are set the other task of seeking in the differences what is common and making it clear beyond all that separates us. The living conversation that is going on in Christendom between the confessions and churches moves untiringly in both of these directions. The person who always sees only one side, only what is held in common or only the differences, is making things too easy for himself. No matter how much in his love for peace he emphasizes only what binds us together or how much in his love for truth he stresses only what separates—neither attitude is a helpful contribution to the dialogue. The conversation rather includes both, and the hard but inescapable task is to allow both to be expressed in the right way. Here, in speaking of Luther's theology of the cross, we cannot make a direct contribution to this conversation within Christendom. We can speak only of what is peculiar and distinctive in Luther's theology of the cross.

1

The great importance Luther attached to it can be seen best in the fact that he made this theology of the cross the cornerstone on which minds are divided and go their different ways when he carried on his great debate with the theology and philosophy of his time in the *Heidelberg Disputation* of 1518. It is the theological counterpart of the posting of the *Ninety-five Theses* in Wittenberg. And if, as some say, the Reformation were only a matter of a quarrel between theologians, then April 26, 1518, the date on which the disputation was held in the Augustinian monastery at Heidelberg, would be the anniversary of the Reformation. In theological importance and effect it surpassed by far the indulgence controversy. But the Reformation was, of course, not concerned merely with theologians' questions, but rather with the whole church, the whole faith, the whole life of the Christian. This was the reason why something so seemingly external as the money indulgence, but which actually led in a straight line to the innermost center of piety, became the stone that started the mighty avalanche. In the *Heidelberg Disputation* Luther dealt with only a part of the whole, though it was the essential theological point. He did so with such convincing power that he won over forever a number of later Reformers of southwest Germany, especially Martin Bucer of Strasburg and John Brenz of Württemberg, who were among the listeners.

In this *Disputation* Luther differentiated his theology from that which was widespread then and still is today. This kind of theology, when it seeks to comprehend God in terms of thought, reasons from the visible to the invisible, from the order and beauty of the cosmos to him who created it, from the great events in history and human life to the spiritual power behind them. But does one really arrive at God in this way? Does one not come out only with an idea of an ultimate cause, a force that caused all things? What does this tell us about the nature of God? Causes and forces are neutral; they produce good and evil, blessing and harm. And it is an altogether illicit simplification to regard only the good and bright features of the cosmos as visible evidences of an invisible power, the power of God, and not also the terrible, sinister forces; only the order and beauty of nature, and not also the struggle, the destruction, and death. This illicit simplification, which imagines that it can make God evident by a simple deduction, Luther calls a theology of glory. It would see God's glory directly in its visible traces in the cosmos. But when it does this it deceives itself, for then it must shut its eyes to many, many things that are not in accord with this divine glory. It must close its eyes to suffering and misery in the world, and to see God in these too is the art of the theology of the cross. No, not in these too, but rather to see God first and foremost in suffering. Or to put it even more precisely, we can become certain of the love of God only in cross and suffering. Once we have grasped it there, then we can also see it elsewhere in the traces of God's love in creation.

But only when we have found him in the *dark* are we sure that we are not relying upon a figment of a dream when we believe in the loving Father behind the created world. In the *Disputation* Luther reminds us of the wonderful biblical story of how Moses was permitted to stand in the cleft of a rock while the glory of the Lord passed by. Then the Lord said, "I will cover you with my hand until I have passed by; then I will take away my hand, and you shall see my back; but my face shall not be seen" (Exod. 33:12 ff.).[3]

The person who thinks he can simply infer from the world and life that God is the giver of meaning is making the attempt to see God's face, an attempt which is always doomed to failure. Where then is he going to find meaning for that which is meaningless? God can be seen only from behind when one has found him in the darkness, indeed, only when one has learned to understand that it is precisely in the dark places of our life that God wills to let himself be found. But how could man ever grasp this by himself? We are so fond of constructing a meaningful world and we feel so comfortable when everything fits together. And therefore we are quite willing to reverence the hidden Master when the world shows us its beautiful and purposeful side. But that God dwells precisely where it is hard to find him and that he wills to speak to us there, that only when we have found him there do we possess him so that he cannot be lost—this only the cross can tell us.

2

The theology of the cross is not a theology which is contrived by the process of thinking. If we followed our ideas of the nature of the divine, we would imagine a quite different God: a great, mighty, victorious, indubitably loving, ingenious cosmic architect. But certainly not a God who allows his messenger, whom he sends for the salvation of the world, to go down to ignominious defeat, to suffer and die innocently. It is a theology that one can derive only from an actual event, or better, that one can believe only on the basis of the passion and the cross of Christ. This was why Luther portrayed the suffering of Christ with such tremendous force. This suffering was not only a horrible physical suffering, as it was chiefly represented in medieval devotional literature in order to arouse our pity. Rather Luther took far more earnestly and consistently than did all previous theology the humanity of Jesus Christ, who suffered on the cross, not only physical pain, but also utter forsakenness and desolation. Augustine and medieval theology and mysticism fought shy of accepting the cry, "My God, my God, why hast thou forsaken me?" as a real cry of the dying Christ; they construed it merely as the intercession of Christ for his suffering body, the church. For Luther, however, it was simply bitter truth that Christ had to endure on the cross the consciousness of being forsaken by God. He was spared none of the trial and temptation, none of the remoteness and absence of God that may be imposed upon men. Indeed, for him who came from the heart of the Father and brought nothing but love to men, it was a more dreadful thing to bear this abandonment than for any other man. For Luther this fact that Christ had to fall into the abyss of Godforsakenness and loneliness, was expressed in the Creed: "He descended into hell." He interpreted this to mean, not an event in space, but rather this experience of utter dereliction of the soul. Nor is this experience confined to the cross; the passion is rather only the awful aggravation and consistent conclusion of the loneliness and desolation that Jesus suffered in his whole life through the deafness and opposition of men and often the misunderstanding of his own disciples. Only occasionally do the Gospels mention this, and Luther commented that "if everything about Christ had been written down, we would read of many a severe affliction. He was a man who from his youth was tormented by many afflictions." Actually he had already died in the garden of Gethsemane before he was crucified, for there he had already suffered death and desolation to the depths. On the cross all of the cross of his life was summarized.

But therefore the meaning of his life *for us* is also summed up in the cross. Christ's dereliction means something deeper than the desolation of any human being could ever mean. In that dereliction he became the brother of the loneliest and most derelict of men. This is the seal upon the love of God. No starry heaven, no marvel of creation, can make us so sure of it as the fact that Christ by the will of the Father took upon himself this uttermost affliction of soul. But while he was obliged to plunge into forsakenness, he was not forsaken, but rather led by God's strong, irresistible hand to the only place where he could become the Savior of the world, right next to all who are desolate in the bottommost hell where man left alone inevitably falls into despair.

Christ's cross and dereliction can help us to overcome our cross and dereliction. If God's love is hidden in the cross, then it is also in our cross. There is where God seeks us most intensely, there he desires to speak to us and assure us that his power is revealed at its mightiest in our weakness. The person who has found God's love here, on the cross, will also find it elsewhere, in the cosmos, in human love. But he who looks for it first somewhere else and not in this hidden center of divine help for the world will founder and come to grief upon the suffering and the meaninglessness of life. We cannot see the face of God, but in Christ, said Luther, God gave himself a "little, near face" which we can look upon.[5] It is a human, suffering face, the face of the Crucified. But in it dwells the majesty of the love of God.

3

This theology of the cross contains the germ of Luther's whole theology, and here he differentiates himself from the theology that preceded him. As we saw in the *Heidelberg Disputation,* the theology of the cross is leveled against all attempts to deduce God directly from visible traces of him in the world and thus in particular against all forms of proofs of God, such as those employed, for example, in Thomist theology. Kant rejected the proofs of the existence of God because they go beyond the province of *reason,* but long before him Luther had made it clear on the basis of the nature of *theology* itself that God must be believed and cannot be proved or deduced in part or as a whole. Otherwise we arrive only at a principle of the origin of the world, but never at the living God, our Creator and Father. When we have found and known him in the human face of Christ, in the dark event of the cross, then on the basis of this certitude we can also see and think of the whole of the world in the light of that face, but not the other way around.

Inherent in Luther's theology of the cross is his whole *doctrine of justification,* his opposition to every kind of work righteousness and every concept of merit. For by this means man desires to point to something that is visible, something he has done, which justifies the pardon of God. Even though in Catholic doctrine the merits are understood as resting upon sacramental grace and growing out of it, they are still something to which man can point before God, even though it be in humility, and for which he can hope to be rewarded. For Luther the very idea of merit itself, however narrowly or broadly conceived, was impossible before God. As far as God is concerned, we can only receive and serve. If we can be wrested out of our reparation from God only by the fact that Christ took upon himself the cross, then there is no room for human merit. Then we can only accept this unmerited love in faith and lovingly pass it on to our fellow men. Luther's phrase "by grace alone" is only another expression of his theology of the cross.

The theology of the cross also contains the roots of Luther's understanding of the *church*. For Luther the church is the fellowship of those who believe in Christ. He used various terms to describe it: the community of saints (i.e., believers), Christendom, the people of God that gathers about God's Word. It has often been felt that there is something vague about Luther's statements concerning the church, that they do not provide any clear boundary lines. There is good reason for this; for if it is real, living faith in Christ that determines whether one belongs to the church, to his love, who dares to draw any sharp boundary lines? There are Christians in all confessions who put their whole trust in Christ and seek to follow him in their lives. Thus the church exists beyond the bounds of the confessions. Luther stated this frequently. It is possible to say where the church exists here on earth, namely, where the gospel, the message of the unmerited grace of God, is purely preached. But one cannot say who belongs to it and we dare not presume to draw its boundary lines. It is in the nature of the church of Christ that it cannot be apprehended in the way that we count the inhabitants of a city or pupils in a school. To belong to the church of Christ requires more than making regular contributions or even attending church without being in earnest about one's faith.

On the other hand, according to Luther, it is possible to say very precisely what the church is not. It is not where it is thought that the external truth can be directly and palpably reduced to fixed, unalterable forms here on earth. This again is only a further application of his theology of the cross. It is for the sake of this theology, for the sake of the gospel, not because of an inborn crankiness or spirit of contradiction, that Luther so passionately rejected an infallible teaching office and a spiritual law which because of its supernatural dignity is set above the worldly. For him both were forms which attempted to lay direct hold upon the divine in earthly institutions. At that time he was not confronted with the office of teaching in the form of the infallible pope, since this was not yet a universally accepted dogma, but rather in the form of the infallibility of councils of the church. Luther freed himself from belief in this, not carelessly, but only after painstaking deliberation. It became completely certain to him that no institution in the church is in possession of the truth by virtue of its office, but that every institution must be responsible to, and prove itself to be valid by, that which is the sole truth, the gospel. It is not the office that decides, but rather the teaching. "He who teaches the gospel is the pope and disciple of Christ; he who does not teach it is Judas and betrayer of Christ."[6] The Reformation rests upon this statement. And when Luther made it, his only concern was to call the church of his time to account for itself before the gospel.

For the same reason he also rejected the idea of a *spiritual-divine law*. Next to the posting of the *Ninety-five Theses* and the *Heidelberg Disputation,* Luther's burning of the canon law (*corpus juris canonici*) outside the Elster Gate in Wittenberg on

December 20, 1520, is the third overture to the Reformation. It was of no less significance than the other two; it put an end to the medieval concept of ecclesiastical law and the relationship of church and state. And again Luther did this not because of revolutionary extremism or for political reasons, but rather in consequence of his theology of the cross. For the idea of spiritual law claims to bind the divine to a definite, earthly, and visible form of church, and hence it is demanded that this spiritual law be respected as being above worldly law. This too is an attempt to possess God directly, to force the eternal into the form of a visible institution. For Luther this was in contradiction to the gospel. If Christ had to allow himself to be nailed to the cross in order to make it possible to believe in the love of God, then the church dare not desire to gain a hearing by means of the authority of an infallible Office of Teaching and cannot claim a supernatural right for itself and its teachings. Christ is not in it where it displays its splendor and power and seeks to secure its position by means of politics or of a divine right, but rather he dwells only in its preaching and its discipleship, which, however, also leads it into suffering. Hence, when Luther enumerated the marks of the true church, he always included—along with the right use of the Word and sacraments, brotherliness, and love—cross and suffering. This can be the suffering of persecution, but also compassion for the world's distresses and sorrow over the sins of the world.

We could go on at length and show how all parts of Luther's theology radiate from this center, from his theology of the cross. From it his theology receives its inner unity and its distinctiveness from the teaching of other churches. But always when one listens to it carefully one will also perceive the common element in the distinctive as well as the distinctive in the common. Both must be taken seriously if one wants to grasp the meaning of the Reformation. We have brought out the distinctive element by reference to a number of implications of the theology of the cross. The common element lies in centering attention upon the cross itself, in the comfort that it signifies for the individual in his need and for the world in its hopelessness. Luther gave the grandest expression to this comfort when he illustrated in the cross the meaning of the whole history of the world in his wonderful exposition of the Magnificat, the canticle of Mary, in the first chapter of Luke. We can bear the ebb and flow of history, its unpredictability, and its seeming meaninglessness only if we entrust it to the God who is hidden within it, in order that he may lead us upon new paths when we no longer see a path at all. The key to this mystery is provided by the cross. Luther said, "Behold, Christ became powerless on the cross, and yet there he performed his mightiest work and vanquished sin, death, world, hell, devil, and all evil."[7] For those who believe, the cross of Christ is the assurance that God's work really begins where, from the human point of view, everything in the life of the individual, the church, or the world is lost.

III

The Meaning of the Church

WHY DO WE always keep talking about the church? Is it really so important? God is important. And the fact that I and all men should become conscious of him as the One by whom we live and in whose presence we live, this is important. Jesus Christ is important because he was the figure in whom God drew near and still draws near to humanity in a unique way. And therefore the gospel, the preaching of Jesus and the preaching about him, and faith in him are important. Renewal by his Spirit, discipleship of Christ, and life in accord with God's will are important.

But the church? After all, it does not exist of itself and for its own sake, but only for the sake of these realities; it is not primary, but only a means. Ought we not to speak far more of the source, more of the origin than the derivative, the means?

In actual practice almost the reverse often seems to be the case.

56

The Meaning of the Church

The church regards itself as important and is looked upon as being important. It does not want to be overlooked, it wants to have its say on the great problems of intellectual, political, and social life. And people expect this of it. More than in some times past, people in public life, politicians, economists, and the molders of culture are willing to listen to what it has to say today. This could be very fruitful if the church were not always falling into the temptation of revolving overmuch about itself and therefore— and also precisely because so much is expected of it—of talking more about itself than of the powers by which it lives and which constitute its sole reason for existence, namely, God, Christ the gospel, and discipleship. In the times in which it suffered persecution and contempt it was often able to speak more effectively and convincingly of these things than in times when it enjoyed universal esteem. This is not a reproach directed against individual persons, but rather an almost inevitable danger, which the church, and everyone who is serious about the Christian faith, must therefore keep all the more firmly in mind.

Hence, it is a salutary thing to see that it need not be so. There are classical documents from the history of Christendom in which the fundamental truths of the faith receive intensive treatment but very little is said about the church. Among these documents is Luther's *Large Catechism,* that protean summary of Evangelical faith, which we shall follow in this discussion. In the *Large Catechism* Luther starts, not with a definition of the church, but with the life of the church. The most palpable intrusion into our existence which has something to do with the church is Sunday. We can pass by the church buildings without ever entering them. But nobody can escape Sunday and its extension, the festivals of the church year. Our public and vocational life is regulated by Sunday. There are, of course, quite natural reasons for this, which Luther clearly stated in his explanation of the Third Commandment:

"You shall sanctify the holy day." It is necessary to interpose a day of rest at certain intervals in order that "man and beast"— Luther does not forget this—"may be refreshed." It was therefore merely a matter of expediency to have the service of worship on this day of rest, since otherwise it would not be possible for people to come together. In giving this natural and practical reason for the choice of Sunday, Luther's purpose was to strip it of everything legalistic, such as the insistence that it be on the Sabbath, the day mentioned in the Bible, and overanxious, scrupulous observance of rest on this day. People could rest on another day if this were necessary. This sanctifying of the day, along with the worship of God, should not be "so narrow as to forbid incidental and unavoidable work." This is intended to be quite as broad-minded and free as it is stated, but only in order to lead us more emphatically from the secondary to the main concern. In his *Catechism* Luther develops two theses concerning Sunday observance which give us a deep insight into his understanding of the church.

1. The meaning and purpose of Sunday consists "not in the resting but in the sanctifying." In God's eyes the day of rest has no value in itself; only the sanctifying of this day, or more precisely, the sanctifying of the person on this day, has value. For Luther there are no holy days, just as there are no holy things or ceremonies or rites or estates (priests or monks). He set himself against a misconceived, objective concept of holiness. One cannot call everything a holy work, he says, "unless the doer himself is first holy. But here [on Sunday] a work must be performed by which the doer himself is made holy, which takes place only through God's Word. Places, times, persons, and the entire outward order of worship are therefore instituted and appointed in order that God's Word may exert its power publicly." Hence there is only *one* criterion of holiness and that is that it be done by and for the sake of the Word of God. In this way everything

we do can be sanctified, even the very ordinary actions which do not occur in the context of worship. The service performed for our neighbor, the work we do in our job, or in the care and rearing of children can be holy in the sight of God. And much that is outwardly regarded as holy can be quite unholy in God's eyes, even if it occurs within the context of worship. And yet that which is holy and pleasing to God, even though it is performed in drab, everyday life, is deeply and inseparably related to the service of worship; for this is the place where God's Word keeps pressing in upon a person in order to sanctify him—for his life on Sunday as well as on weekdays.

2. Luther sharpens this first thesis by adding a second: "God wants it [Sunday] to be holy to *you.*" A Christian might easily say, "After all, I not only observe Sunday, I also sanctify it. I go to church." Very well, but what about Sunday being holy to *you?* He who does not come home from worship sanctified has not sanctified Sunday. To be sanctified naturally does not mean to come home as one who is radically renewed, one who has been transformed into a saint. This would be an illusion and hypocrisy. But to be set in motion by God's Word in the depths of one's being, to be appalled at oneself, more confident in one's trust, more hopeful and assured in one's suffering, more resolute in one's love—this surely is the way a Christian should come away from Sunday, from the service of worship or his own quiet meditation of the Word of God. Then he has sanctified the holy day— or more properly, then the holy day has sanctified him.

Through these thoughts of Luther concerning the holy day we have found the determinative dimension from which all the action of the church acquires its meaning, namely, *sanctification.* And sanctification not primarily as a demand made upon us, but rather as the totality of God's willing and working, so that we must first pray to him: "Hallowed be thy name." The church's only purpose is to help us in order that God's name may be hallowed in our life. It is noteworthy that the sanctifying or hallowing of the name of God, or we may say, our sanctification according to the will of God, is not presented to us merely as a command, "Be a respectable person," but rather as a petition to God himself, "Hallowed be thy name." God's answer to this prayer is the gospel, and the instrument of the gospel is the church with all that is entrusted to it, the Bible, preaching, instruction, works of love, the sacraments, pastoral care, and whatever else it does, on Sundays as well as on weekdays.

One could therefore describe the meaning of the church, not only on the basis of the Commandment to sanctify the holy day, but just as well by reference to the first petition of the Lord's Prayer, "Hallowed be thy name." Here again we find the same distinction: God's name is holy in itself, we cannot take away from God any of his holiness or add anything to it. The only thing that matters is that God's name become holy to *us,* that it become manifest in *our* life that we are giving glory to him. Here again we touch the nerve of all the preaching and action of the church, the nerve of all that is Evangelical: You are the one that is meant; not God, not the church, not the observing of holy days, not the celebrating of holy rites. "Hallowed be thy name" always means: Hallowed be thy name through me. This is the way I must pray. And this is also the way the church must pray, and this sums up all it does and says.

And therefore the church really belongs in the third article of the Apostles' Creed, the article of the Holy Spirit—or as Luther called it, the article of sanctification. For what it is concerned with is not a doctrine of the Holy Spirit, a part of trinitarian doctrine, but always with us men and that we be sanctified. "To sanctify is nothing else than to bring us to the Lord Christ." Or as Luther puts it more precisely in speaking of preaching of Christ: "Where

Christ is not preached, there is no Holy Spirit to create, call, and gather the Christian church." This beautiful, simple phrase of Luther, "to bring us to the Lord Christ," sums up the whole activity of the church, its behavior toward people as well as what it says to them. And this lays its claim also upon those who are not ministers in the church. We are all ministers of the Holy Spirit, whether we are clergymen or laymen. It is true that the preaching in the public service of worship is a special function for which one must be trained and called, but it is only a part of the far more comprehensive calling that applies to all of us, namely, to bring others to Christ.

Therefore Luther, if we look at his definition of the church, emphasizes that it is not an institution founded upon holy offices. It is rather founded upon the solidarity of believers, the fact that they belong together under their Lord Christ. The various offices in the church grow out of their common calling which sends them out to those who have not yet found Christ. Luther illustrates this by reference to the parallel term for the church in the third article of the Creed: "I believe in . . . one holy Christian church, the community of saints." And when he speaks of the community of saints, he is not thinking of the departed saints whose intercession is invoked in the Catholic Church, nor does he mean that the members of the church are holy people. The saints are rather the believers who know that they are sinners and that they need forgiveness. The very moment a person is convinced that he is really a quite passable Christian who has demonstrated this through a Christian life, he thereby excludes himself from this community of saints.

With his predilection for etymology Luther seeks to make this clear by examining the meaning of the words. The word "church" seems to him to be subject to misunderstanding, because one always thinks first of a building which is declared to be holy because it has been consecrated; again that false, objective, material holiness. He therefore would if at all possible avoid the word "church." Even the word *ecclesia* which is used in Greek as well as in Latin is better. As Luther rightly saw, this word originally meant something quite secular: a regularly called assembly; in this case, called together by God's Word and composed not of citizens but of Christians, not a civil community but a Christian community. This reminder of the originally neutral meaning of the word again serves the *one* fundamental thought which we can always trace in Luther, namely, that the real nature of the church lies not in something external, not in a consecration, a hierarchy of offices, a sacred building, or in holy rites, but in something inward, in faith, in love, in sanctification, only in the fact that it brings men to Christ.

If we keep this in view, then perhaps we will understand the brief statement in which Luther sums up what he wants to say about the church: "I believe that there is on earth a little holy flock or community of pure saints under one head, Christ; called together by the Holy Spirit in one faith, mind, and understanding, possessing a variety of gifts, yet united in love without sect or schism."

Or perhaps we still do not understand it. ". . . in one faith, mind, and understanding . . . yet united in love without sect or schism"—is not that simply in flat contradiction to reality? Does not that statement incomprehensibly ignore what is certainly an obvious fact, the many divisions in the church? And here we need not think only of the great confessional divisions, between the Eastern church and the Western church, between the Roman Church and Protestantism, and between the many Protestant churches. Is it not also true that within every individual church there are so many differences of opinion and tensions that these statements concerning the unity of the church are simply given the lie? Did Luther fail to note this? Certainly not. Even before the Roman Church excommunicated him he was deeply troubled by the differences and divisions within it: the theological antagonisms, the power struggles among the monastic orders, the popes, and the bishops, the rift between the passionate reformers and those who did not see that the church needed a renovation in head and members. And he was equally troubled by the fact that in the new reformed churches, too, differences and schisms again appeared. But he also knew that nothing can be done to prevent this through the coercion of church law or by external means, but that this only hardens the differences.

There has never been such a thing as an externally visible unity of the church of Christ, not even in primitive Christendom. The New Testament gives us very clear glimpses of the differences and tensions that existed in the apostolic and post-apostolic period: Jewish Christians and Gentile Christians, those who adhered to the Jewish law and those who knew they had been freed from it, advocates of highly speculative Gnostic teachings and those who stood for a very simple Christ-gospel, parties that fought for supremacy in individual communities, as shown by I Corinthians. And there was no council, no conference of bishops, no universally recognized apostle, no pope, no ecclesiastical statute book to which appeal could be made. No congregation had precedence over the others; they rather constituted, as has been rightly said, an "ecumenical fellowship," bound together solely by their common confession of the Lord Christ, by their common worship and a life of discipleship that led all the way to martyrdom.

So Luther did not say: I see one church which is of one faith and full of harmonious love. What he said was: I *believe* that such a church and its unity are a matter of faith, something in which we believe. This does not mean that I believe that this or that organized church is the only true church of Christ. It means

63

rather that I believe that beyond all the differences and divisions among the churches there is *one* Church of Christ, the community of "saints," of those who believe in Christ, who hear his voice and follow him, and want to bring others to him.

Such persons are to be found in all churches. The sphere of the Holy Spirit is wider than that enclosed by the walls of the confessions. The church is illimitable but not invisible. It has visible and audible gifts and goods: the gospel, the proclamation, the sacraments, works of love, the evidence of suffering overcome. As Jesus said, it is known by its fruits, not by its law; its forms of organization, its rites, not by its verbal creeds, however orthodox they may sound. This is not to disparage the confessions; it does not render meaningless their struggle for a right understanding of the gospel. For decisions of the question of truth always lead inevitably to divisions. But the many churches, every one of which is human patchwork, like everything else that is earthly, are over-arched by the *one* church of Christ in which we can believe. The rule by which that one church lives is that we permit ourselves to be sanctified as true Christians through God's Spirit and that we bring others to Christ. The more the churches in which we live as separated brethren are governed by that rule, and everything else beyond this rule becomes unessential, the more they are really the church of Jesus Christ.

IV

The Sum of the Reformation

THE OLDEST Gospel, the Gospel of Mark, in its first chapter sums up the proclamation of Jesus in the following words: "The time is fulfilled, and the kingdom of God is at hand; repent and believe in the gospel." If the Reformation was a renewal of the primitive Christian gospel, as our forefathers and we Evangelical Christians today are convinced it was, then a test of its genuineness would have to show how the message of the Reformation accords with the sum of Jesus' proclamation in these four compressed statements.

The renewal of the primitive Christian gospel is not repristination or repetition. There is no repetition in history. Accordance in great historical relationships does not consist in mere recitation of past formulas but rather in new appropriation in view of the questions of one's own time. Appropriation, to be sure, is genuine only if the fundamental truths are not violated, changed, or shifted by additions. We are therefore concerned with agreement in these original truths as we compare this summary of the message of Jesus with the message of the Reformation.

The time is fulfilled—the kingdom of God is at hand. These are two statements concerning the historical hour, or more precisely, one statement. For Jesus did not proclaim: The time is ripe for me to appear, as the revolutionaries cry: It is time to put an end to the old social order, it has long since been ripe for it; or as the dictators say: It is time to establish order and curb all these confused opinions and interests with a strong hand; or as we say for political or economic reasons: Europe is ripe for unification. Jesus was not thinking of such human conjectures, which can be right or wrong, but which in any case are always subjective and uncertain. He did not listen to the voice of the times in order to find in them the justification of his appearing. He listened to the voice of God that said to him: The time is come, go, preach, and suffer.

God's hour has come, this is what Jesus means when he says, "The time is fulfilled." And only because it is God's hour does it become his hour. The concentrated attention of the Reformers was focused upon this hour. Their whole concern was to understand this unique hour of Jesus Christ, this center of time. Luther was therefore deeply disappointed when in his struggle for this understanding he was always confronted with arguments from tradition, church discipline, and the dicta of the church fathers. "I cry: the gospel, the gospel, Christ, Christ. They answer: the fathers, the fathers, the usage, the usage, the statutes, the statutes."[8] His sole concern was the voice of Christ and the apostles' witness to him. After the church had strayed far afield, he called it back to its source and origin. But this origin is not a historical beginning and thus something in the past. Christ is the center of time and this means that through him God has spoken in every time. Luther therefore devotedly searched the Old Testament for traces that point to Christ. Therefore he thought of Christ in his own time as the Living One who is nearer to us than the long chain of transmitters of tradition and Church Fathers that lies between us historically. Every generation faces him anew and immediately, and Luther wanted to regain this immediacy to Christ for his own time.

If Christ is living and present, then this means that for *every* historical epoch the time is fulfilled. God's hour is always striking. But someone must hear it striking. Jesus heard it in the solitude of the wilderness. Luther heard it in the quietness of the monastery. Without quietness the striking cannot be heard. But Luther heard it in a way different from that of Jesus. It was his hour, but for him it was so in a sense totally different from Jesus. For him it was the hour of Christ. It was this hour alone that he desired to serve and to engrave once more upon the heart of Christendom, and by doing this to serve the hour of God. In this he himself was nothing, nothing more than the voice of one crying in the wilderness. He did not thereby become a new center of time, like Jesus Christ. On the contrary, he was only calling Christendom back to its lost center.

The Bible calls prophets those who have the courage to pass on the wakening call of God to their own time. It did not mean by this—as our eroded language would often make it appear— people who prophesy or predict something, not soothsayers, but truthtellers. These prophets are the most important people in history. The world emerges from times of chaos and disorder only because from time to time God sends it prophets: Isaiah, Jeremiah, Augustine, Francis of Assisi, Luther, Calvin, not to mention the minor prophets who live in every age. Napoleon's dictum that politics is our fate is not even half true. What is more true is that man is the fate of politics. What counts is not the quantity of power and economic forces, but rather what we do with them. History at its deepest is not political history or economic history, powerful as these forces are, but rather spiritual and intellectual history, which means human history. The prophets stand in full opposition to those who put the mind and soul in the service of power, the virtuosos of mass psychology, the demagogues, the organizers of public opinion. For the prophets seek not their own, not their own dominion, not the triumph of their own idea. Rather God's dominion has come upon them and they proclaim to their time nothing else but the dominion, the kingdom of God.

The true prophets, however different they may be in personality and in time, bear common, unmistakable features. Their course begins in the bottommost depths and again and again leads them through the darkness of despair. "Ah, Lord God! Behold, I do not know how to speak. . . . O Lord, thou hast deceived me, and I was deceived. . . . I have become a laughingstock all the day. . . . If I say, 'I will not mention him, or speak any more in his name,' there is in my heart as it were a burning fire shut up in my bones, and I am weary with holding it in, and I cannot." So cries Jeremiah.

"How often my heart trembled and pounded and reproached me: Are you alone wise? Are all the others in error? Have so many centuries been in ignorance? What if *you* have been wrong and dragged so many others with you into error and eternal damnation?"[9] So Luther once described the *Anfechtungen,* the doubts, the uncertainty, the misgivings which were constantly assailing him.

The word of the prophets always begins with themselves. "Woe is me! For I am lost; for I am a man of unclean lips," Isaiah confesses before the face of God. "I knew a man," says

Luther in a veiled reference to his struggles in the monastery, "who claimed that he had repeatedly suffered these punishments, only for the briefest moments of time, it is true, but so severe and so much like hell, that no tongue could adequately express them, no pen could describe them, and no one who had not himself experienced them could believe them."[10]

Then the word of the prophets always goes on from themselves to the community of God, to Christendom, not against those outside, not against the conditions of the times. It is so easy to complain about the spirit of the times, the general irresponsibility and indifference, the materialistic attitude of other circles. And it is so hard to begin with oneself, in one's own house, one's own congregation and church, and there expose the fact that faith is not being lived. The Reformation differed from the many reform movements of its time in that it began from within and moved outward. Luther began at the innermost of things, with living, immediate faith in Christ, and ended with the outermost, with the financial maladministration and extortion of the church by the Curia. And only after he had dealt with the church did he go on to the wrongs and abuses among the people and in the state. If *Christendom* does not hear the striking of God's hour, then all the summons and shouting at the times are fruitless.

And finally, one last thing that made the prophets prophets. The voice of God which they heard drowned out all the other voices that pressed in upon them: rejection, despair, derision, hate, and threats. So it was with the prophets of the Old Testament. So it was that Luther stood before the Diet of Worms, seeing this spectacle of power and hearing, above all the voices that would daunt him, only this one voice that kept saying: It is neither right nor safe to go against conscience. He therefore refused to make the demanded recantation. "Even those who are weak in faith can disregard the voices of the world with closed ears. But who will close our conscience that it may not sense the judgment of Satan and of God?"[11] He was not, as many thought, an enemy of the Roman Church—he said on one occasion—"for I sincerely love not only the Roman but the whole church of Christ. But I also know that one day I shall die and will have to give an account of the truth at the return of our Lord Jesus Christ, whether I have spoken it or kept silent . . . I am responsible to the Lord for the Word, however unworthy I am."[12]

The piercing, overwhelming voice of God which they hear gives to prophetic persons the courage to face the mighty of this world, and what is more, the courage to endure the accusations and assaults of their own hearts: "Are you alone wise? What if you have been wrong?" Then the voice of God is not only a command but also a stay and a certitude. After describing this dreadful doubt: What if you have been wrong? Luther goes on to say, "Finally, however, Christ strengthened me with his sure and faithful words, so that my heart no longer trembled and pounded . . . as one can laugh at the threatening storms from a safe harbor."[13] It is not human courage and defiance that make men prophets, but rather this certitude experienced in the midst of all outward and inward trial, the certitude that comes from above. By this alone do they dare to say to their own time: The time is fulfilled—God is at the door—the kingdom of God is at hand.

This is what the Reformation said to its time. And if we hear its message, this is what it says to our time. We have pretty much forgotten to mark this note in the message of the Reformation. For the most part we say that it gave us justification by faith or the return to the Scriptures, freedom from human and ecclesiastical intermediaries between God and us, freedom of conscience, and therefore a freedom and self-responsibility of spirit. All of which is true and right. And yet it all remains incomplete, and even fundamentally wrong, if we do not direct it to the goal that sums it all up: In all these things—in justification and freedom —God is calling us anew to his rule, his kingdom. God does not will to leave the world as it is. Today he is still calling to us, in order that with us and through us he may change the world. One day he will change the world without us. We do not know when that day will come. But it is not the measure of time that matters. The important thing is that we know that he is near, that he is behind the veil before which we live, behind the time, the brief time, that is ours. We are not afloat in infinite space; everything we do is very finite and final.

We understand this perhaps somewhat better than earlier generations, which seem to us to have been rather carefree and lighthearted, because they had not yet gazed into the abyss of the possible self-destruction of mankind. It is not inescapable and we therefore pray that it may not happen. But it is tremendously near. Today we do not need any mythological concepts of the future; we can say scientifically how the world could end. This would be a nihilistic idea of the end of the world, if we do not know that in every end God comes, the God with whom there is no end, but only his eternal kingdom which is always incomprehensibly renewing itself. And this is something that cannot be visualized. There is only one thing that can help us to envisage it and that is the nearness of our own end. War and air raids, which most of us still remember, traffic deaths and the sudden collapse of overworked men, have given us a clear enough picture of how quickly the end can come. No generation before us ever heard such a message and preaching of death. But do we hear it? Or is its endless repetition too monotonous for us? Have our ears become deaf? It is not too hard to open them again and at least hear this one thing: We do not have unlimited time, neither we ourselves nor Christendom nor the world. God is very near.

Then the questions begin to throng in upon us. What about your life? Has it brought forth fruit, or did it never get beyond mere starts, intentions, and half measures?

Christendom, what about your commission to go and teach all nations and what about our Lord's saying: By your love shall you be known as my disciples (John 13:35)?

What about mankind? Has it any meaning and purpose? Or will everything it has created, thought, willed, and suffered end in the abyss of self-destruction?

If we allow ourselves to be touched by these questions, we shall again understand better why this message of the fulfillment of time and the nearness of the kingdom of God stands at the center of the primitive Christian proclamation. It also stood in the center of the Reformation message. Here the two agree.

This realization gave the Reformers a profound consciousness of history. When a man knows that he does not have much time left, he may react in two ways. For those who think they have to be the masters of their own fate and do everything in life themselves, it may cause a great urgent unrest that keeps them rushing through the rest of the time left to them, and thus they really do lose it.

For others who know and can say, "My times are in thy hand," a great peace may enter their lives, a peace which is not only tranquillity but concentrated power. Everything becomes so much more genuine, so much more earnest, when it is seen in the light of the end. Colors become more luminous and human encounters more intensive and meaningful. Life becomes fuller again when we stop hurrying past one another like shadows and never availing ourselves of conversation, lightly assuring ourselves that we shall meet and reassuring ourselves when the meeting never comes. When we take time seriously, it suddenly spreads out marvelously. We learn to live in the present, instead of merely skimming through it. Though our outward time may elapse, there is an inward time that grows as outward time decreases.

It was in such a feeling of fulfilled time that the Reformers lived. As hardly any other person, Luther yearned for what he called the "dear Last Day," on which God will put an end to all dividedness, all struggle and suffering and the dominion of sin and death. Full of joy, he hoped that the new fresh sweep of the gospel in the world, the great throng who flocked to proclaim it, the martyrs who bore witness to it in their death, were harbingers of the great coming of God. But he also knew that with God there are no measures of time, that God's hours can pass by, that this may perhaps be God's last knock upon the door for his people. The gospel can move away like a passing shower, as it has passed over other countries which are now pagan.

So, out of deep joy and deep concern, Luther gained the incredible energy and capacity for work that changed his age, indeed, the world. It is his capacity for work that is borne in upon us as we look at the more than one hundred stout volumes in which are gathered only the literary fruit of his life of hardly more than thirty working years. And yet every word in them is contemporary, full of sparkling life, a life that was conscious of the brevity of time and the nearness of God.

This consciousness did not lead him to the kind of resignation that says, What is the use? But rather to the utmost straining of his powers, not away from the world, but out of the quiet of the cloister into the struggle of the world, in order to make the most of these hours of grace while the gospel was still available. For God's kingdom demands the work of human hands. It is therefore not only a future thing but always here in the present. The eternal begins in time. Here is where the decisions are made. And this too is entirely in accord with the New Testament.

In the Reformation view, the kingdom or the rule of God embraces three things: *man, the church, the world.*

Man, the whole man—the decisive and distinctive feature in the Reformation concept of man is that it always sees man standing before God as a totality. When we men look at ourselves without looking at God we dismember ourselves into parts and strata such as body and soul or body, soul, and spirit, the classical distinctions which sound so primitive to us today. We make far more differentiations: instincts and cognitions, inherited and acquired characteristics, fixed fundamental functions and free play, bondage to childhood experiences or impressions and autonomy, volition and inhibitions, good endeavor and debilitation, individuality and psychological type, natural constitution and cultivation, free formation and the given physical organism, and so on. This is the way we have to speak, dissecting and dismembering and after analysis again synthesizing, when we talk about man humanly, psychologically, and philosophically.

Luther did not dismiss this, but before the eyes of God what matters is something else, the whole man, whom God claims for his kingdom, our self, which before God is indivisible. Before God I cannot divide myself into a higher and lower self, a spiritual and unspiritual self, into vices and virtues, sins and good works. In his eyes I am always a unity. *I,* not something evil within me, am the bearer of my evil thoughts. *I* am the bearer of my longing for the good, not some good impulses within me.

Luther once stated this with deep insight: "It is the whole man who loves purity and it is the same whole man who is pricked by evil lusts. . . . This is the glorious thing about God's grace, that it makes us enemies of ourselves."[14] That expresses more profoundly the wholeness of man and the conflict within him than does Goethe's idea of the two souls in the breast of Faust which are trying to separate from each other. For the truth is that it is always *one* soul that sells itself to God or to the devil, to love of neighbor or to Mammon. The other soul, which we are so fond of distinguishing from it, is always there too. We are always an I, a whole person. And God lays his hand upon this self, this whole man, and he wants the whole of him. The kingdom, the rule of God, means not merely a strengthening of the good impulses within him. It is not merely an increasing of his good thoughts and deeds, a curbing of the physical, the animal part of him. It is not a flight into the intellectual or spiritual, an avoidance of the perils of the world. Rather God sets the whole man into rebellion against himself. God wants his whole soul; he wants him with all his mind and his body, his thoughts and his deeds, his faith and his love.

These last two, faith *and* love, are definitely included. It is a dreadful misunderstanding to think that Luther required of the Christian only faith and not also love. The first book he wrote of his own full choice and not because some external occasion demanded it was his *Treatise on Good Works* (1520). In this book his aim was to teach real good works, the works of love that flow out of faith, out of gratitude for God's goodness and forgiveness. Love is response to the love of God in which we have faith. Love is the expression of our faith that is turned toward our neighbor, as inseparable from it as our reflection in a mirror is inseparable from us. We have no faith if we have no love. But we come to love only from faith; we do not come to faith through our efforts to love. Faith and love together constitute the whole man as God would have him to be.

The second point: *God's rule over the church.* When the Reformers were asked to state the goal of their struggle, they said that it was directed against the rule of men in the church and the thousands of rules and precepts made by men. For them the rule of men was the papacy with the great legal power which it claimed for itself, especially the rather unsavory Renaissance popes of their time, who were more concerned with politics, waging wars, art, and their splendid courts than with the proclamation of the gospel and the salvation of the faithful. Luther's own trial, which was dragged out for years for political reasons, was a striking evidence of how spiritual questions were obliged to give way to the worldly interests of the Curia and the Pontifical State. The rule of men—this also applied to the bishops, who for five hundred years were at the same time worldly, often very worldly, princes. But it was also true of the complicated, almost unsurveyable legal structure which had been erected over the simple truths of the gospel.

To Luther, as he once said, the gospel appeared to be an eagle imprisoned in his cage. And when he proceeded to set it free, to make room for the voice of the gospel above everything else, he discovered that he was not being fought and refuted with spiritual weapons, but that this whole legal machinery was set in motion against him, with all its disciplinary measures, demands for unconditional submission, the banning and burning of his books, the demand that he be delivered to Rome, and finally excommunication and the imperial edict imposed at the behest of the church. We must keep in mind what it meant for Luther that the attitude of the church toward him exactly confirmed the picture of it he had previously gained. He therefore labored all the more passionately at the task of seeing to it that everything that was said and done in the church be set under the light of the gospel and tested by the Bible.

But let us not forget that the rule of man in the church was not confined to the forms of it that existed in the Roman Church of that day and against which the Reformation was directed. It is a continuing temptation of the church, all churches, including our own. Again and again it has appeared: bureaucratic rule, the rule of princes, the rule of theologians, the rule of parties, the rule of certain classes or groups, political ideas and interest, strong and ambitious personalities, the rule of scrupulosity, dead forms, and customs which we mindlessly drag along with us.

The church, or better, we as the church are always in need of fresh reformation, and we should not be afraid of it. No church should be afraid of it. The most salutary thing that can happen to it is when there rise up within it men who have heard the knocking of God whose will it is to bring the gospel to new sovereignty in his church. Just as God's claim to sovereignty sets man in revolt against himself, so these invasions of the divine Word and Spirit from the outside are the disturbances that keep the church from dying. These invasions of God's Word and Spirit cannot be confined and channelized into legal forms. They do not come from appointed officers and teachers. God's receiving Spirit does not always come from above, but often from below or from the side, sometimes from one and sometimes from many at the same time. This rests with God: We can do nothing but open our ears and listen intently in order to hear the striking of God's hour and at the same time be careful that we do not make of it a new rule of men and again let life slip from our hands.

And finally, *God's rule over the world*. This never means the church's rule over the world. It is the greatest temptation of the church to confuse these two. When it gets the idea that it must exercise its rule over the world in the name of God, it is actually evading the rule of God within its own sphere. God has his own way and his own means of keeping the world under his rule. And this too was the Reformers' concern. For they saw how quickly the church loses its soul when it succumbs to the temptation of power, whatever form it may take. It has another service to perform.

The rule of God over the world means rule through men. We

are not speaking here of the almighty works of God in creation or the incomprehensible turnings which occur in the course of history. These are unfathomable mysteries which we can only accept and reverence. What we mean is that rule by which God wills to curb and control the destructive forces and preserve order in the world. It is a rule that will be contested until the Last Day and must be constantly re-established; for God does not compel us, but calls us to serve him in freedom. So he exercises his rule through us men. "Fill the earth and subdue it"—this is God's call to us to share his rule.

If the earth could speak, what would it say we have made of this dominion? The forests which for centuries we have senselessly chopped down and turned into desert; the birds and animals which have been dreadfully decimated and sometimes almost extermi- nated in order that men might wear their feathers in their hats, possess their furs, grow rich with ivory, or enjoy for money the inglorious thrill of hunting the remnants of African big game. Or the mysterious constructive and destructive forces in matter which we have discovered and from which we have fashioned the most ghastly weapons of destruction. The earth, the birds, the animals cannot speak. But others can speak and have spoken, and they will go on speaking: slaves, the victims of the Inquisition, the galley slaves, the women burned as witches, child laborers in mines and in factories, the hungry and exploited proletariat of the last century or the inmates of concentration camps, oppressed and persecuted peoples and races, people who have been turned into parts of a machine in a soulless political system in our own century—these and many others accuse us and will go on accus- ing us for what we have done with the rule that God has en- trusted to us.

God's true rule over the world is therefore both a protection of the world against man and protection of man against men. And this protection he has also entrusted to us men, to the guardians of public order, law, and social justice. But we must also not forget the first, the earliest bulwarks of this protection and this order: the parents. We are all appointed to serve this rule of God over the world.

Many of us are parents and all of us are citizens. And every citizen is appointed to be a guardian of public order, not only the officers of justice and the police. We are so prone to transfer this bit of entrusted co-responsibility to others, to professional people. We do this as parents to the school, which, after all, can provide only a modest, though often valuable, aid toward true, innermost education. As citizens we turn this responsibility over to state and legal bodies which, after all, are made up only of human beings who have a particular point of view, a limited function and authority, and above all are able only to cure symptoms. We shall gradually recover health only if we all again realize in whose service it is that we exercise protective rule over the world. All of us, parents and citizens as well as professional people, politicians, jurists, teachers, social workers. In his many writings on political and public life, Luther earnestly and passionately enjoined this responsibility upon the conscience of the people of his time and upon us today. Nor can we shift this responsibility upon the church, upon experts as it were in matters of conscience. We cannot expect that it will provide us with directives on political or social questions any more than in scientific matters. It can and it must keep us alert, give good counsel, entreat, and warn. But in these matters it has no higher warrant from God than that which is given to every one of us who are in the service of his rule over the world.

God's rule—over men, over the church, over the world—is always the *rule of love*. God recognizes no other way of ruling. And this above all is what the churches, what we as Christians, have to say and exemplify to the world. The great proofs and demonstrations of love are the demonstrations of the hidden, still struggling, still contested rule of God: a Friedrich von Bodelschwingh gathering the misery of epileptics around him and giving them a chance to live a human, secure existence; an Albert Schweitzer giving up scholarship and music to serve sick and stricken Negroes in Africa; Christians of both confessions sealing with their lives their love for their country and their faithfulness to their Lord in the resistance movement; and Abbé Pierre taking upon his heart the distress of the homeless poor in Paris.

Love is interconfessional, nor does it stop at the borders of Christendom. Gandhi is a great example of this. Wherever love and sacrifice are actually "lived," there God's rule is at work. For us Christians this is only a call to love more fervently, more completely. For we know that he first loved us, and what we can do is only a response to his love, a discipleship.

The Gospel of Mark summed up the proclamation in four statements. So far we have dealt with only two of them: "The time is fulfilled, and the kingdom of God is at hand." Is it necessary to dwell at length on the other two: "Repent, and believe in the gospel"? We have been talking about them all along. They are the natural conclusion from the message that God's hour has struck anew.

The Reformation was a movement of repentance, not a movement to change the organization of the church, to improve the service of worship, to cleanse the church of all kinds of abuses, not merely a new theology. Rather it began with repentance: "When our Lord and Master Jesus Christ said, 'Repent,' he willed the entire life of believers to be one of repentance," declares the first of Luther's *Ninety-five Theses*. The hallmark of all real revival movements in the church is that they always begin with repentance.

The Sum of the Reformation

And this is how the Reformation must be understood, not as the bold revolt of a contumacious monk, but rather as an earnest, beseeching call to the church to turn around and repent. Not until that call, which shocked so many individual Christians and theologians, failed to receive a hearing among those who were responsible, did Luther's indictment take on the piercing sharpness which is familiar to us in the Old Testament prophets and the words of Jesus spoken against the scribes and the Pharisees. But then later Luther spoke in the same terms to his unrepentant congregation in Wittenberg and assailed the contempt for God's Word in Germany just as severely as that in the Roman Church. His concern was with the rule of God, which can be frittered away and lost.

And yet the last statement, "Believe in the gospel," is actually the real, authentic message of the Reformation. How could Luther, without despairing, ever have launched his call to repentance into the world of hard hearts, which are always in the majority, if he had not been sustained by God's unwearying assurance of his love for the world? But with it, how could he grow weary and despair?

This assurance sounds like a strong connecting note, through the message of the prophets, of Jesus, of the New Testament, and of the Reformation. It is only this assurance that gives to their call to wake up and repent its heart-gripping power. It is a note of praise that spans the ages like an arch: "Blessed be the Lord God of Israel, for he has visited and redeemed his people." The hours in which God wills to re-establish his rule are in truth the hours of visitation in which God comes anew to meet his lost sons. This gospel keeps the world young, as long as God allows it to live. That is the sum of the message of Jesus. That is the sum of the Reformation.

V

The Abiding Validity
of the Reformation

THAT PART OF history which we Evangelicals call the age of
the Reformation is in Catholic usage generally called the age of
the schism. Is that a mere trifling distinction? Are they not merely
two different aspects of one and the same historical event, both of
which are correct? In the term "Reformation" the emphasis lies
more on the origin, in the term "schism" on the result. Does it
make any difference, then, whether we call this age one or the
other?

The question leads us to the center of the discussion of the
meaning of the Reformation at that time and the question of its
significance today. If what happened then was only a schism,
then the obvious question is: Is it not time to put an end to it?

The Abiding Validity of the Reformation

After all, today there is more at stake than the existence of a confessional church. Christianity as a whole has been challenged to a decisive battle with an atheistic-materialistic view of the world, which is to say, a negative religion. For materialism supports its denial of God with an almost religious fervor, with the certitude of a doctrine of salvation. "Why should there still be division, why schisms?" said Pope Pius XII at Christmas, 1949, at the inauguration of the so-called holy year, and then proceeded to invite the separated to come back home to the Roman Catholic Church. One must understand how natural this question is to Catholic thinking—if what happened four hundred years ago was nothing more than a schism.

If we listen to the question seriously and with understanding, we are compelled to make it very clear why what happened then is more than a schism, why it was a reformation.

1

In the late Middle Ages and the sixteenth century there were many reformations. The word, which for us today denotes a definite period of history, then signified a process which by its very nature was always unfinished and in need of repetition and one that covered all possible areas. Man spoke not only of a reformation of the church in head and members, a demand which grew louder and louder in the fourteenth and fifteenth centuries, or of a reformation of morals, but also of a reformation of the empire, for which many proposals were made, such as the famous *Reformatio Sigismundi* at the time of the Council of Basel (1431–49). Men spoke of the reformation of monastic orders and cloisters, the reformation of municipal laws in which piece by piece the Roman law was incorporated, the reformations which were undertaken, often at fairly frequent intervals, in the universities, such as the reformation of the University of Leipzig in 1502, prompted by the rival establishment of the University of Wittenberg a few days before. Even Luther's bitter opponent, Duke George of Saxony, demanded at the Diet of Worms in 1521 a "general reformation" through a council of the church.

For Luther and the other "reformers" it was something altogether reasonable and natural to work for a renovation of the church. For them—and this we must keep clearly in mind—it was a vital process which the church needed then and requires again and again. They did not even claim the term "reformation" as their own. The word appears only occasionally in Luther's earlier writings and then only in the sense of the general reformation which the church needs. Not until the seventeenth century did retrospective historians speak of the Reformation in the sense in which the word is used today.

Of the many reformations only one remained as *the* Reformation and became a term for an epoch in our historical thinking. This is not a mere whim of usage which may be explained by the fact that many books were written about the Reformation of the church, which then provided the title for this whole period of history. Nor was it only because the Reformation of the church was the most important, most comprehensive, and most far-reaching of all the reformations and thus, in the eyes of those who came later, absorbed the other reformations and remained the classical Reformation. Rather it is because the Reformation became something different from what it was originally intended to be: not something uncompleted and repeatable, as is every reform in every area, but something completed and therefore unrepeatable. New churches arose, something which Luther never wanted, independent, fixed structures, separated from the old church, whose reformation was the only thing that Luther cared for. And the period in which these churches came into being naturally constitutes a definite historical epoch.

Thus the terms "Reformation," "Reformers," "Reformatory," became terms descriptive of an epoch. But hidden in these terms the original dynamic meaning of reformation lives on: the renewal of the church, of all churches, of the whole of Christendom, and continual renewal in every time that it is necessary. This is important. If the churches of the Reformation ever forget that they sprang from this never-ceasing purpose of renewal for the whole of Christendom, they will have become unfaithful to their original task. The term "schism," however, lacks this determinative, total church meaning of the Reformation, as well as the idea of the renewal of the church, whether it be its need for renewal or also the concern and endeavor to renew it. It therefore conveys far less of the meaning and purpose of this epoch than does the term "Reformation."

2

Why is it that the Reformation has become something other than what it was originally intended to be? When we say "Reformation" we do not mean only the personal events and experiences in the faith of Luther, although the Reformation movement did not begin anywhere else except in the monastery cells in Erfurt and Wittenberg. Nor is the Reformation only a new theology, although the new theology was the driving force behind the great upheaval. The Reformation is rather the whole far-flung historical event that arose in the spiritual struggles of an individual and then—like everything historical—had visible and tangible results in the life of one nation after another. This total historical event of which we are here speaking and which divided and still divides the church today, embraces all the individual views of the faith that distinguish us.

This break in the sequence of history brought about by the epoch of the Reformation occurred at that moment when Luther was excluded from his church because of his criticism of the theology and the ecclesiastical conditions of his time. It was *his* church from which he was excluded, for it was for no other church that he uttered his fervent pleadings and prayers and his painful laments and angry indictments. Everything he did and said and wrote was not against it, but for it, for its sake, not in order to establish a new church. It was because *his* church, the Roman Church of that time, excluded him that an inner reform, which had often taken place before, became something new, outside of the hitherto existing church, namely, the irrevocable and unrepeatable Reformation.

The exclusion was based upon the fact that Luther declared that he could not blindly submit and begged for refutation, for evidence that he was in error. His church did not refute him, however. The reasons it put forward for his condemnation were more than inadequate, as Catholic theologians even then and more than ever in recent times have admitted. Instead of answering him, it demanded obedience. And this Luther could not yield without having been refuted. In his constantly repeated offers to defend himself on one point after another Luther never left any doubt that he could not recant unless that which he saw as the truth were proved to be wrong by the Holy Scriptures.

In this conflict two worlds, whose opposition to each other has become absolutely fundamental to the whole intellectual life of modern times, collided: on the one hand, a conviction which insisted that it was found solely to the known truth, and on the other, an ecclesiastical body which demanded unconditional obedience and recantation. We would be oversimplifying the conflict if we were to say that on the one side was conscience and on the other only the act of obedience. No; according to the Roman view, for every theologian who deviates from the teaching of the church it is an obligation of conscience to subordinate his own opinion to that of the church. And not only because the church is older and its thinking is more comprehensive, but rather because, according to the Roman view, the promise of infallible truth has been given to its teaching office. When Luther was summoned to recant, without even an approximately adequate attempt having been made to refute him, an appeal was also being made to his conscience, or more precisely, to his faith that the truth had been inviolably bestowed upon the governing courts of the church.

The conflict that led to the break was therefore not merely between conscience and obedience. It arose rather out of a profound difference in the concept of truth. On the one side there was a truth which was itself discerned from the Bible and was therefore willing to defend itself and be refuted. On the other side there was a truth, the foundation of which is not reasons—not even biblical reasons about which one could dispute—but rather a truth that demands faith in the church's possession of the truth, which Catholic Christians must be completely willing to muster beforehand.

In the collision of these two worlds the modern age, with all its strengths and its stresses, the age to which all of us belong and which has so often been declared dead and yet is still very much alive, was born. Naturally it came out of many different preparatory factors and by many paths. But the decisive encounter in which blow was given for blow, so that what came into being was not something half, but something new and whole, took place in the various stages of Luther's life. The first was in Augsburg in 1518 when Luther declared his readiness to defend himself in any form and implored Cardinal Cajetan that he be refuted wherever he had erred. Then finally the break ensued when the Curia promulgated its bull of condemnation against Luther without any argument and without any refutation of Luther's condemned statements, which were in some cases presented in jumbled form and torn out of their context. This bull executed the break between the church of that day and Luther; and Luther could confirm it only by refusing to submit and symbolically declaring the bull a nullity by burning it.

Luther's refusal to recant did not spring from defiance, arrogance, or pride, as it has often been misinterpreted. He could not recant without being convinced of error. For him this would have been a betrayal of the truth. And to remain silent concerning the wounds and abuses in the church would for him have been a betrayal of the church.

The division in the church therefore did not arise over this or that individual point of doctrine, however important it might be, such as indulgences, the sacrament of penance, justification, the sacraments, the sacrifice of the mass, canon law, etc. At all these points Luther had introduced a renewal of theology, from which much might perhaps have made its way in time. The conflict which transformed the Reformation from a reform movement into an event which was the beginning of a new epoch was not a matter of individual details but rather of the whole, of the Roman church's whole concept of itself.

The truly tragic thing was that the Roman Church of that time, concerning whose religious and theological infirmity even sober-minded Catholic scholars are today agreed, was misled by its demand for faith to condemn Luther before it had heard him. Precisely because it was not equal to Luther's tremendous earnestness and theological power, it was so tempting to it to demand obedience and recantation without discussion. By immediately applying this weapon and using it almost solely, the Roman Church forced the movement of renewal, which it so urgently needed for its theology and its life, to become a separate church. Luther never desired this and therefore took this unavoidable path only reluctantly and hesitantly. It was not only a lack of interest and skill in organizational questions that caused him to begin rather late and cautiously the building of new congregations, but more because he did not want to block the way to a reform of the whole church. His thoughts were and continued to be directed solely to this end.

The Catholic Church, because it immediately excluded Luther, reaped only a few of the fruits of this renewal and those only in a hidden way. With all the friendliness and fairness with which individual Catholic theologians frequently evaluate Luther's historical purpose and his personality today, the church itself confronts him with hands that are tied—tied by all the authoritative condemnations since 1520. On the Roman Catholic side these condemnations prevent the church from really taking seriously or actually accepting anything of the thought with which Luther wanted to renew the church, including the Roman Church. The apparatus of canon law was immediately set in motion against Luther instead of dealing seriously with him for several years and testing the truth of his criticism and his understanding of faith. This has had its consequences down to our own day. And in doing this the Roman Church broke asunder the unity of Christendom a second time, the first time through its excommunication of the Eastern Church in 1504, which was pronounced carelessly and without considering the consequences, and then through the excommunication of Luther in 1520. It thus inflicted wounds upon the body of Christendom which have not been healed.

3

Now, of course, there can be no doubt that a separation between Luther and the Roman Church would have had to come sooner or later. For, after all, the central question was this: Is the church, automatically and without being subject to examination, in possession of the truth, or may it be tested, indeed, *must* it be tested, by the Holy Scriptures? Recantation or refutation? But a lot depended on this "sooner or later." Instead of receiving any hearing at all for some of the ideas of his theology and being able to contribute to the church's self-examination, Luther was forthwith driven out of the church and along with him all those who had long yearned for a thorough reformation of the church. Thus for the time being the rich, fresh stream of new religious and church life, which arose with astonishing quickness, flowed past the Roman Church. And after thirty years when it set about to begin laboriously and reluctantly to make the necessary theological and ecclesiastical reforms in the Council of Trent, the lines had become too rigidly drawn for the old church to have been able to receive from the Reformation movement any immediate gains worth mentioning.

The separation was of course unavoidable as long as the Roman Church refused to give up its claim to infallible truth and unconditional obedience. And Luther could never agree to this. And even in the more recent Catholic works, such as those of Joseph Lortz, for example, which evaluate Luther with greater understanding of the purity and profundity of his religious motives than did the earlier Catholic historians, it is quite rightly seen that the fundamental rift lay in the question of the teaching authority of the church and still remains there. This is where all discussions of individual Catholic and Reformation doctrines, which have or ever can be held, end.

When Luther refused to accept the judgment of the pope concerning the known truth of Scripture, he was still able to do so—this we dare not forget—in the consciousness that he was not thereby violating the unity of the church. For in his conviction as well as that of many others in late medieval times, not the pope but the council was the supreme court of appeal of the church. Even Charles V threatened the pope with an appeal to a council in 1527. When Luther was banned by the pope, Luther was able to appeal to a council, knowing that he had a good right to do so. He did so as early as 1518 after the hearing in Augsburg and frequently in later years, primarily, no doubt, in the hope of getting a better hearing from a total representation of the church than from one man, especially when that man had as little understanding of theology and as little interest in a reform of the church as did the vain and pleasure-loving Leo X. Later the Evangelicals repeatedly appealed to a council, for example, in the Protestation at Speyer in 1529, but, of course, with ever-diminishing hopes. Even from a purely legal point of view—apart from the decisive questions of truth—Luther could in good conscience refuse to submit to the condemnation of the pope alone. When he burned the papal bull outside the Elster Gate in Wittenberg, the unity of the church, which Luther has often been accused of destroying, was not at stake. True, in every case he put the truth above unity. But this was a case in which by this symbolical act of confessing the sole truth of the gospel he showed the pope what his limitations were and reminded him of the supreme court of appeal, the council. According to his well-founded conviction, the truth of Scripture and the law of the church itself were on his side.

4

This is different today. Since that time the Roman Church has gone through a process of development issuing in the principle of papal absolutism. According to the established canon law today, an appeal from a papal decision to an ecumenical council is forbidden. A person who makes such an appeal is regarded as a heretic and forthwith incurs the severest form of excommunication, and a university, a chapter, or similar community is placed under an interdict, a prohibition of all sacramental functions within its confines. The great dogmatic decisions of the pope, such as the dogma of the immaculate conception of Mary in 1854 or of the ascension of Mary in 1950, were decreed without a council, whereas for a millennium and a half the councils had defined the dogmas. And even if such a definition of dogma were again to be proclaimed at a council, it would not affect the validity of such a dogma, since the infallibility which the Roman church claims for itself is concentrated in the infallibility of the pope— an infallibility above that of the councils, which in late antiquity and in the Middle Ages had been regarded as infallible. The truth is dependent solely upon his decision. And this is the foundation of the demand for unconditional obedience to the doctrinal decisions of the pope. Therefore today we are no longer faced with the same problem as Luther, but rather with the more sharply defined question of the validity of the Reformation over against the doctrine of the Roman Church, which is based upon the absolute, infallible authority of the pope.

The question of infallible authority is not merely one question among others discussed between the confessions; it is rather the pre-eminent question. It is the broad moat beyond which rises the wall of individual differences in faith. Naturally, it was not the question that provoked Luther's personal struggle in the monastery; there it was the question of salvation. The question of authority, however, inevitably became the primal question of the *Reformation,* namely, the historical event through which the revival movement that Luther strove for became an independent church. It is still the pre-eminent question.

5

This can be seen in recent history above all at two points which are important for the fundamental and practical relationship of the two confessions. The first is the dogma of the bodily assumption of Mary into heaven proclaimed in 1950. Though the substance of this doctrine may be strange to us and thus any discussion of it may appear to be fruitless, the fundamental significance of this dogma is even greater because it throws light upon the way in which doctrines are formed within the Catholic Church. Even in the Catholic Church nobody with any education in theology or history can deny that the dogma of the bodily assumption of Mary into heaven was never represented either in the New Testament or within the church until well into the sixth century. And even after that time it existed for another thousand years only in various legends on the extreme margin of the teaching of the church. Karl Adam, the Roman Catholic theologian, has quite correctly said: "Not until the sixteenth century did the ascension of Mary become a subject of church teaching."[15]

When it was declared to be an infallibly true dogma, binding upon all believers, this was a departure from the idea of tradition hitherto held by the Roman Church. Before this time tradition was understood to be something that goes back to the time of the apostles and was handed down from generation to generation. In 1546 the Council of Trent defined it by saying that the truth is "contained in written books and unwritten traditions which were received by the apostles from Christ's own mouth or transmitted as it were from hand to hand by the apostles themselves under the inspiration of the Holy Spirit and thus have come down to us."[16] Now in the place of this concept of tradition something else became manifest, namely, the church's consciousness of faith, a living and continuing thing. This broke the connection between the doctrine of the church and the Holy Scriptures and its historical continuity with the earlier church. In the discussions that took place at that time a Catholic theologian wrote: "The primary standard of my Catholic faith is by no means the Holy Scriptures,

93

but rather the living consciousness of faith of the church of Christ as it exists today."[17]

The church's living consciousness of faith, however, becomes the truth only if it is declared to be true by the verdict of the pope. The issue between Evangelical and Catholic thought today is therefore no longer the old and much-discussed question of Scripture and tradition at all, but rather the question of Scriptures and papal authority. Pius IX was thoroughly consistent when he said at the Vatican Council, "I am tradition." The proclamation of the dogma of the assumption of Mary, which is not substantiated either in the Scriptures or in the hitherto existing sense of the tradition of the church, confirmed what he said.

The second point at which the self-understanding of the Roman Church today becomes especially evident is its attitude toward the ecumenical movement. We can hardly realize today that it was only a few decades ago that the Christian churches came together for the first time in an ecumenical meeting in Stockholm in 1925. Out of that meeting came a movement. If we were to distinguish between our epoch and earlier epochs of the history of the church, we would say that today we are living in an ecumenical age, in the beginning of an experience of Christian unity beyond the bounds of the churches and confessions. Above all the differences in doctrine, faith, forms of worship, peoples, and continents there shone something of the New Testament promise of one flock and one Shepherd. And this happened in the same decades in which mankind macerated itself as never before in its history in two insane world wars. The monstrous hate that was connected with it was not able to kill the love and the yearning of Christians for fellowship, but on the contrary only aroused and strengthened it. In the midst of the dreadful, world-rending antagonisms Christians experienced something of that homeland in which they know themselves to be bound to one another beyond the frontiers of nations. And from this visibly growing unity of the church of Christ the Roman Catholic Church has hitherto excluded itself. It has been repeatedly invited to the ecumenical conferences and it has repeatedly declined. Though broad circles within the Roman Church feel and have expressed the yearning for fraternal ties and a meeting beyond the confessional bounds, the church's authority has always said no. It goes without saying that it could not say anything but no, because its claim to be absolute will not permit it to recognize anything but unconditional subordination.

What then are we to conclude from all that we have tried to clarify? Should we simply conclude that nothing has changed, that the separation is the same as it was four hundred years ago, and that the right of the Reformation to hold to its own way remains unchanged? This is certainly not correct. Nevertheless we do not want our reflection upon the fact that the Reformation was intended to be something different from what it became because of its exclusion by the Roman Church to be in vain. If we lose sight of the original meaning and purpose of the Reformation, its sense of responsibility for the whole church, we will betray the heart of Luther in the Reformation. He never strove to found a new church, but only to call for the renewal of the whole church of Christ. And in these four hundred years this original goal of the Reformation too has remained unchanged.

By no means does our recollection of the historical nature of the Reformation end in resignation, in marking out again the old boundary lines. True, the rift is still there. Every Christian who sees things soberly and clearly knows this. And if he is a real disciple of Jesus, no matter whether he is a Catholic or an Evangelical, he will look upon it only with pain. Indeed, the rift is in a sense even harder to bridge than it was in Luther's time, since now the infallible authority has passed from the representative body of the church, the council, to the pope alone. Now there is no court of appeal beyond him to which one could turn. We Evangelicals can only say no to this understanding of the nature of the church, just as the Roman Church, as long as it holds to this fundamental claim to the truth, which rules out all discussion, can only say no to the fundamental nature of the Reformation.

But seeds can fly over the broadest moats. For this we are glad and we thank God that he has ways where we as human beings see none at all.

We rejoice at everything the Roman Church has experienced in the way of inner and outward renewal since the sixteenth century—which, as those who are familiar with history know, would not have happened without the powerful impetus of the Reformation—renewal in the doctrine and the life of its clergy, the elimination of abuses in the Curia and in the money indulgences, the deepening of its theology and its piety.

We rejoice that in the Catholic Church for several decades the Bible is being read to an extent which would have been inconceivable in the sixteenth century. Now, despite the reservation of doctrinal authority, we can talk with each other about the Bible differently from ever before.

We rejoice that Evangelical hymns are being sung in the Catholic Church and would wish only for the sake of our coming closer together that Catholic congregations were more clearly aware that these are Evangelical hymns which they are singing.

We rejoice at the deepening and refinement of understanding that comes through the liturgical movement.

And we rejoice above all at the vital theological conversation which has come into being between the churches, the mutual giving and receiving that is taking place, and in particular the willingness that is being shown to evaluate Luther himself more justly and to examine his theology in order to verify its truth content.

If we cannot honestly rejoice at all this, we have lost sight of the original goal of the Reformation, the renewal of the church of Christ.

In saying this we are not laboring under the illusion that in these questions the concerns of the Reformation have been fulfilled and thus that its task is finished. This is not the case in any of the areas mentioned; everywhere differences and contradictions remain.

The interpretation of the Bible is not free and subject solely to judgment of known truth, but is rather bound to ecclesiastically approved translations and interpretations and in disputed questions is subject to authoritative decisions, particularly those of the papal biblical commission.

The liturgical movement has not fundamentally changed the meaning of the Roman service of worship, particularly the sacrifice of the mass, but has only combated the excrescences of liturgical life.

Even in the newer, more deeply biblical Catholic theology the Pauline doctrine of grace and justification has by no means been given the dominant centrality which in our judgment it deserves according to the New Testament. The controversy between us over this goes on as it did at the time of the Reformation.

And even the most understanding of Catholic Reformation scholars are still not thinking of granting that Luther was right in his cause, in his theological opposition to Rome.

So it is with almost all the questions which were in dispute at that time. And others have been added, the significance of which did not become wholly discernible until after the Reformation, especially the question of Mariology which has since gained tremendously in importance for Catholic theology. And yet, despite

97

all these differences, the seed can and does fly over the moat that separates us, and it flies both ways. It comes in our direction too. We must test without bias everything that comes across to us in the way of experience of faith, the living of the Christian life, and theological insight and gratefully accept it if we can reconcile it with our understanding of the New Testament message. The wide fundamental rift between us and the abiding indispensable validity of the Reformation dare not prevent us from doing this.

But good seed can be carried by the wind only if good fruit has grown first. Ultimately, it all depends upon this, and not upon demarcating the boundaries and protesting. Whether we are the church of the Reformation—even with regard to the Roman Church—is measured not by the loudness and theological correctness with which we profess the Reformation, but solely by how much fruit of confident faith and active love we really bring forth. It depends upon whether we ourselves are a living church, whether every congregation is a living congregation, which even Catholic Christians regard with respect. As Christians and as a church of today we must not be too quick to equate ourselves with the church of the Reformation.

When we say that we are convinced that the right of the Reformation to its independence over against all invitations to reunion with the Catholic Church, which once pronounced the exclusion, remains unchanged, this does not simply mean that *we* are right. It means that Luther is right, that the Reformation is right, and that it is also right compared with us, if we are not a living Reformation church. And finally—in full accord with Luther's spirit—the Bible is right, the gospel is right, even against the Reformation wherever it has become unfaithful to it.

The end result of a study of the Reformation dare never be the complacent conclusion that we are in the right and that everything is in order among us. The result must rather be a solemn concern whether we are always ready and willing to allow ourselves and our church to be renewed by the Spirit of Christ. This is the never-ending movement that Luther wanted to arouse. This is the abiding purpose and the abiding validity of the Reformation.

VI

The Reformation View of God

THE REFORMATION VIEW, the Reformation picture of God—can
one really speak in such terms at all? A picture is always something circumscribed, it has its fixed outlines, it always represents
something that our eye can take in and is therefore only a seg-
ment. Can one speak of a "picture" of God? We do not mean
the question in the sense of whether one can represent God in
painting or sculpture, but in a deeper sense: Can one express
God intellectually in a metaphor or a picture, in the image of the
Father, the King, the great Architect of the universe, indeed, can
he be grasped at all in any human concepts, graphic concepts such
as these we have just mentioned or nongraphic such as the ultimate cause, omnipotent power, inextinguishable light, eternal
love, etc.? After all, these are all human concepts which do not
touch that which is incomparable, God.

100

If there was ever anybody who sensed the mystery of God, it was Luther. He made some remarkable statements which one would never expect of him. "Nothing is so small but God is still smaller, nothing so large but God is still larger, nothing is so short but God is still shorter, nothing so long but God is still longer, nothing is so broad but God is still broader, nothing so narrow but God is still narrower." This is not the kind of statement one would look for in Luther, but rather in pantheistic thinkers like Giordano Bruno, the Renaissance philosopher, or in modern nature mystics. It states something we can no longer formulate in conceptual terms; it confesses that in God all concepts and all contrarieties are dissolved and abolished. It speaks, or perhaps it would be better to say, it stammers about the mystery of God.

And the mystery of God includes the mystery of the world. The world is full of God. It was not merely given a nudge by God from the outside, so that now, as Goethe says, it goes on twirling about his little finger; it is rather full of God, full of his ever-present life. If he is the Creator, Luther once said, "then he himself must be present in every creature, in its inmost, outermost being, around and around, through and through, below and above, before and after, so that there can be nothing more present nor more inward in all creatures than God himself with his power." Luther almost tumbles over his own words in order to drive this home to us: God is the life of the whole and every part, he is in the cosmos and in every individual, in every creature, "deeper, more inwardly, and more present than is the creature himself." God is nearer to me than I am to myself. And as he is in me he is also outside of me, in the trees and leaves, in water, fire, and stone, but in exactly the same way also in the ebb and flow of history. He is in the triumphs and defeats, the fortunes and misfortunes, the rise and death of nations. He acts through the men of history. They are his "veils," his "masks," as Luther was wont to say. He not only sends these men, he does not merely allow history, any more than the universe, to unfold after he has set it in motion, but is in the midst of it, very near to it, indeed, he is himself the life of nature and human history.

Incomprehensible mysteries! They are the truest of realities, but we cannot grasp them, either in pictures or in concepts; we can speak of them only in faltering, contradictory intimations. And yet we must speak of them. For this knowledge of the mystery of God, which is beyond us, is the deepest thing that binds us together as men, indeed, that which really makes us humans in the first place. Therefore the men of all times and all religions have sought to speak it, as well or as poorly as they were able. We cannot refrain from speaking about it because, in so far as we are really human beings, we are all affected by it and must be made conscious of this which we hold in common.

But what does this knowledge of God's mystery mean for me personally, for my life? God is nearer to me, we said, than I am to myself. Is this a comforting or a frightening truth, helpful or devastating? That depends upon whether I know who this God is. Who is behind this mystery? The tree, the stone, the fire tells me nothing about that, nor does the storm that we feel sweeping over us in history tell us anything. What we learn and experience in history is conflicting and ambiguous. Times of splendor and prosperity are by no means only times of blessing for the nations. Times of suffering can bring blessing, but also despair, ruthlessness, and indifference. It always depends on whether we hear the personal call of God in it, or whether we believe that the wheel of a blind fate, of anonymous, incalculable forces, is passing over us. And this distinction decides everything.

Who must distinguish and decide here? We ourselves. Here that which binds us all to one another as a dark sense of mystery suddenly becomes altogether personal. Here the question is whether I can say that this God of trees, stones, and the confusion of history is *my* God, the Lord of my life, who knows me and loves me and guides me.

But how can we say Yes to this in the face of the impenetrable darkness that surrounds God? Surely only if out of this darkness a voice says Yes to us in order that we may say Yes to him. I would wish that this should not be taken as a piece of persuasive piety. We cannot reach this truth by a flight of feeling. On the contrary, the first thing we must see soberly and clearly is that every mere flight of emotion ends in a void and never wrests God's secret from him. "Brother," said Schiller, "a loving Father must dwell above the starry skies." He *need* not dwell there, but he does. He *need* not exist. Human thought can never say that he does. It can just as well be a cold blind law that dwells above the stars. But Schiller's "must," with which our emotion is so fond of allowing itself to be carried away on the wings of Beethoven's music, is not really his statement at all, but only an echo, a weakened echo of the gospel. Without the Christian message, which has gone out over the world for more than a thousand years, he could never have said it.

The real content of the gospel and the Reformation proclamation is that the mysterious God acquires a face. In order that we might say Yes to God, he first said a personal Yes to us. Personal —this means, in order that we can grasp and understand it, through a person, through a man like us, through Jesus of Nazareth. Again and again Luther pictured this miracle with great power and inexhaustible warmth, the miracle that for our sake God made himself small, took on a face, entered into a human life and lot. The face of God that gazes upon us through the human face of Jesus has lost none of the impenetrability that surrounds the Ground of the world and the Sustainer of all life.

103

It is wonderful how Luther was always able to express with the same power both the mystery of God and his face, his picture in the image of Jesus Christ. Never does he forget the one in speaking of the other.

> He whom the world could not inwrap
> Yonder lies in Mary's lap.

Both are equally true, the wide world and Mary's lap, the remoteness and the intimate nearness, eternity and this bit of historical, earthly life through which God speaks to us.

What he wants to say to us is something very personal, something that every one of us needs as the ultimate and determinative help for our life. And what he says is this: Trust; do not be afraid—this message of the angel is the beginning and the end of the gospel. Do not be afraid of the forces of nature, of fate, of the stresses of life, of sickness and death, of men, of yourself, your sins and weaknesses, your failures. I am behind them all, in the midst of all. Have faith and trust, I will help you.

He subjected Jesus to the extreme test, the ultimate dereliction, where only the ultimate, outreaching trust could ever hold on. Nobody could ever be more sincerely tried and tested than he was. And therefore he is the only one who can help us to trust in the face of the mystery of God that surrounds us and which we all feel.

VII

The Reformation View of Man

WE HAVE SPOKEN of the Reformation view of God. It encompasses the tremendous span between the God who is the hidden life in tree and fire and water and human history and the God who comes to us in human form in the man Jesus Christ. The two are inseparably one. Out of the hiddenness comes the personal Word which says to every single one of us: Trust. Such trust can be ventured only by the individual himself. Nobody can argue him into it or take it off his hands, and he cannot supply it for another. This brings us, then, to the concern of this chapter, the Reformation view of man.

The fact is that in dealing with the Reformation view of God we have already said something very basic about man. Almost all of us sense something of the mystery of God that surrounds us. The very fact that man is aware of this mystery is what makes him a human being over against other living beings. Even the primitive religions are evidence of this. There is hardly a man who is so dull and brutish that he has no sense of this in his heart; perhaps this would more likely be true of those for whom the inebriation of civilization and technology has burned itself out and who therefore have no feeling of a higher order above them. They are indeed lower than the animals, who, though they do not will or know what they do, nevertheless live in their inviolable order. But let us leave them out of account. By and large we may say that this sense and feeling of the mystery in and above the world and his own fleeting life is inherent in man as a man.

And this is also the view of man held by the Reformation, by Luther. It is not true that Luther, as many think, dreadfully exaggerated human sin and regarded man as utterly godless. On the contrary, in his beautiful exposition of the Book of Jonah he pointed to the pagan mariners on board the ship with the prophet when a storm arose as witnesses to the fact that there is a sense of God in the heart of man. "Each cried to his God" (Jonah 1:5). This proves, said Luther, that they have some presentiment of God even though they are pagans and have altogether different gods. But more than that, they even know something about him, namely, that God is he who can help in the sea and in all the distresses of life. "This light and understanding is in the hearts of all men and it cannot be quenched or extinguished." Luther therefore did not ridicule the prayers of the heathen; he took seriously the spontaneous prayers which arise directly from need and distress. However imperfect they may be, they nevertheless go in the right direction.

And yet it is a long way from such a cry of distress sent out into the dark, to the deep unshaken trust that sees the face of God in the midst of the darkness. We all sense something of the mystery of God, but seldom do we take the step toward faith. And only when we take that step do we find ourselves with God himself, the God who finds us in the darkness and speaks to us. And this leap from surmise to faith is what the gospel, what the Reformation, is about.

Then too, man has a conscience. Even though there are many who have stifled its voice within them, it is still inherent in the being of man. And who could guarantee that he can really and finally choke it off? It can happen, and it has happened innumerable times, that a seemingly dead conscience may begin again to speak very clearly and persistently. It is a part of what makes us human beings men. For Luther and the Reformers it was the most important endowment of man. The message of the gospel cannot be spoken to an ultimately conscienceless man any more than to the devil. When Luther stood before the emperor and the diet at Worms and at the risk of his life refused to recant, the reason he gave was that it is neither right nor safe to act against conscience. He who acts against conscience has God—and sooner or later himself—as his enemy.

Indeed, man has more than that which we usually call conscience. Luther was deeply convinced that down in our hearts we know that we exist to love. We live by love—there no one who has not received love and with it the best thing in his life, from parents, husband or wife, friends, or whatever else. But therefore we also live for love. Love is an unending stream. It grips us, but if we do not let it carry us along, we are like the mud in the bed of the stream. All of us sense something of this, unless we have become less than human. Luther made no distinction between the words, "As you wish that men would do to you, do so to them" and "You shall love your neighbor as yourself." For we need love from one another, and therefore we must give love to one another.

And finally, God gave us our reason with which to subdue and structure the earth and order our life together with other men. It is quite wrong to think, as is sometimes done, that Luther had no regard for reason. The sharp words he said about it are directed only against the use of reason where it does not belong, in our relationship to God. This relationship is beyond all reason; there it has nothing to say. But where it does belong, in our relationship to the world and men, there Luther praises it as the greatest gift of God. Without reason there would be no law and justice, no scientific knowledge, no education. It is a kingly thing in man, indeed, Luther can say it is something divine in him. And it is also something vital and living. Luther frequently said that the laws which are written or fixed in some other way are not sufficient. Often it is only the free, living reason which can find the way to true justice.

This is man—furnished with the finest organs which are capable of showing him the way through life, indeed, the way to God. He possesses a sense of the sustaining mystery of God, a conscience, a knowledge that we live by our mutual love, a reason by which we can order our life together peaceably and justly. Luther was convinced that these organs are so deeply inborn in man that we can and must address and appeal to him on the basis of these endowments. Otherwise he would no longer be a man. But does man live in accord with the counsel of these organs? In reality he lives for the most part in a way that is godless, conscienceless, loveless, and without reason. The gifts which God has given to him rise up as his accusers. Only when we see this high view of man, which the Reformation too proclaims, do we see the dreadful truth. Only then do we see the terrible judgment that it pronounces upon man, the sinful man who has lost God.

In the Cathedral of Chartres, among the numerous small sculptures over one of the side portals, there is one that shows God the Creator and behind him, only partially emerging, the first man. He is still half covered by God, as it were between nothingness and being. The eyes of both are looking in the same direction, their faces are unmistakably similar. The little sculpture is often called *Adam dans la pensée de Dieu,* Adam in the mind of God, Adam as God thinks of him. This is the only true view of man, God's view of man whom he conceived and created, the view of man as he is in reality. And this view from above is the concern of the Reformation. It is the judgment that we hear in the Bible, the bitter question, "Adam, where are you?" or the lament, "I do not do what I want. . . . I can will what is right, but I cannot do it" (Rom. 7:15 ff.), the lament of the man who knows that God is looking at him.

The upward look strips us of every possibility of comparing ourselves with one another. Naturally there are differences among us men, differences in degree of self-control, ability to love, patience, and so on, and we are capable of making some progress in these things. But when we look above, these degrees of difference become meaningless. The man who knows that he stands beneath the eyes of God also knows that all the abilities and gifts only obligate him the more: "To whom much is given, of him will much be required" (Luke 12:48).

Therefore Luther cleared away all the differences and distinctions which he found in his church, the lower and higher degrees of perfection and holiness which can be achieved through monastic life or ascetic disciplines, the compulsion to perform individual good works by which to improve one's status before God. This is not what matters before God. Before God man is always a unity. This is Luther's fundamental contribution to our view of man. I cannot separate myself into higher and lower, spiritual and unspiritual, divine and demonic. *I* am the bearer of my evil thoughts, not something evil within me, an evil part of me. *I* am the bearer of my yearning for the good, not some good impulses within me. Luther stated this profoundly: "It is the whole man who loves purity, and the same whole man is excited by evil lusts. . . . Thus it is that man fights against himself. . . . The glorious thing about God's grace is that it makes us enemies of our own selves."

This insight of Luther into the wholeness of man was also a psychological discovery of the highest importance over against the ancient attempts to divide man into body and soul or body, mind, and soul, The self is always inseparably one, but the self can also be set in rebellion, in rebellion against itself. But this can be done only by something that comes from the outside, by God's law that awakens, by the gospel which helps us to become more and more free from our old self which has turned away from God. We say "more and more" because this rebellion lasts through our whole life. But God says that we are this now and wholly. He no longer regards the past, he cancels it out as we are never allowed to do, he forgives it all. To believe this, to let this light of the gospel into our hearts—this is the beginning of the new life. Then the gifts which God has furnished us take on new meaning and power: the sense of the mystery of God above our life, the conscience, the ability to love, the clarified, helping reason. But all this not from within ourselves but solely through God's re-creating power. In his gracious eyes, which look at us in the face of Christ, we are again what he wanted to make of us: a new creature Adam as God thought of him.

VIII

The Reformation View of Life

THE REFORMATION VIEW of God and the Reformation view of man are bound together by a common characteristic. They are both concerned with the *whole God* and the *whole man*. Not with only the God of nature or the God of revelation, but with him who is both ineffably mysterious and humanly near in the figure of Jesus Christ. And Reformation thinking is concerned not only with our better, our spiritual self, which would seek to distinguish itself from our lower urges and passions, but with the whole man, body, soul, mind, and instincts, who has turned away from God and whom God would turn back again to him. And therefore Reformation faith—this is the conclusion we now must draw—is concerned with the *whole* of life. Faith is not concerned merely with a religious or spiritual sphere, separated from our other activities, from vocation, business, technology, politics, etc., but rather with life in all its breadth.

Anybody who has reflected about his life at all has surely faced the question: What is my life after all? The never-ending routine of work that rules our days, year in and year out? The sum of all the constantly recurring tasks that often make the life of a house-wife so wearisome? The struggle to exist, to get ahead in life, which so quickly becomes our merciless master, consuming all our powers? Or is my real life the little area which I keep free for other things, for books and art and music, for the meager family life which in so many cases is left to us today? Or, just because we so seldom experience these joys today, is my true life really only that innermost realm of the soul into which I enter once in a while, in prayer, in church, in reading a Bible passage, in lifting up my heart to the starry heavens or to some other marvelous spectacle of nature? I believe there are two things we all feel when we face this question: how poor we would be with-out this realm of mind and beauty, these experiences of joy and quietness—and at the same time, how poor we would be if they were all that constituted our life. If this were so, it would mean that a hopeless rift would run through our life. The place where we live our real life would be terribly small.

The gospel aims to set the whole of life in the light of God. Just as God is in all life, in trees, flowers, and animals, in the ebb and flow of history, and in every individual destiny, so he is with me and above me everywhere in my whole life. We are not now going to talk about the faults, failures, delinquencies, and sin which the light of God can reveal in our life. With a bit of honesty we are quite able to see these things for ourselves. Rather let us be reminded that in the light of God our whole life is full of opportunities to bring something of the life of God into the world. We are constantly coming into contact with people, in our families, our jobs, and other encounters—a never-ending chain of opportunities to show some kindness, patience, concern, some evidence of love. Strictly speaking, there are no neutral encounters between people. Every meeting has something in it at the moment which either binds people together or separates them. In every encounter we either turn toward the other person, with a bit of courtesy, politeness, and warmth, or we turn away from him, with indifference, disregard, and coolness, which we perhaps may hardly be conscious of but is felt by the other person. How true this is we sense when we meet a warm and pleasant person whose voice and face and gestures even when uttering the most trivial words betray this concern for others. God loves us through people. True, he also has direct ways of showing his love for us, but mostly it comes to us through people. When we withhold our love from others, we contribute toward destroying the bond with God in them.

And our life in our vocation is likewise a chain of opportunities to carry something of God's light with the darkness or the twilight of the world. For many people today it is not always easy to come to terms with their vocation in life. Our economic life is so specialized that many vocations, especially technical jobs, are nothing more than partial functions in what was formerly a whole. They demand only certain skills, not the whole man. But even in the case of many other callings, which demand more of the whole man, we often see that they are being regarded only as an opportunity to make money. The calling becomes merely a "job." And that reduces it to emptiness, and at this point where we are obliged to give the most time and our best strength our life becomes empty. Then one day comes the inevitable question: What really is my life?

There is no universal remedy for this deep-rooted distress. It is so different in different people, and there may also be cases in which it is really incurable and can only be borne. But I believe that something decisive has already happened when a person realizes this, just as healing begins with knowing where one is sick. There is a deep disorder in our life if our vocation is only a matter of making money. Our word "calling" or "vocation," like so many others, owes the profoundest meaning it has to Martin Luther. He took a word, which hitherto had what was primarily a religious meaning, that of a call from God, and applied it to our worldly state, our work. The older use of the term still survives in the Catholic Church today when it speaks of the vocation to the priesthood or to a monastic order which a person experiences in his heart. Luther expanded this usage of the term, and now for all of us, Protestants and Catholics, who speak the German language, the word *Beruf* has acquired a deeper meaning. Every vocation, every job, is a calling, something committed to us by God. Luther saw that the worldly stations in life have the same value in the eyes of God as the religious. A faithful worker or farmer is of no less value to God than a faithful pastor. Therefore Luther used the same word "calling" for all positions.

We must hold on to this deep meaning of the word "vocation." We cannot change the technicizing and the division of labor in modern industry and the specialization of many jobs. This is largely, though perhaps not always, inescapable. But it is a help to know that wherever we are and whatever we do there, we have a charge from God. When we ask ourselves what this is, naturally we shall have to express it very differently in different vocations. But for all of us there are two things that are required of us in our vocational life: faithfulness and humanity. Our German people have not yet recovered from the grievous spiritual and mental diseases which they went through in the last decades. They experienced one fever after another: the despair of the miserable years after World War I, the nationalistic delirium of

114

the Hitler years, the giddiness of victory and the paralyzing fear during the war, the black hopelessness of the collapse, the pain of banishment and expulsion, the destruction of countless lives, the hard-bitten rage to work, and the frenzied urge to earn money. These are all symptoms of illness and fever, the effect of which will continue for a long time to come. If our people are to grow sane and healthy again, it will require quiet faithfulness in our work whatever our calling is. We do not need consuming zeal, breakneck speed—this produces at most only a fleeting success—but rather the conscientious care with which we do our work, whether it is recognized or not. And along with faithfulness, God requires humanity. In every vocation there are countless opportunities to see the human being in the other person and to treat him as one who has been given to us by God. We need only ask ourselves how we would like to be treated as persons, then we will have the key to how we should treat others.

So far we have discussed love and our work as the two essential features which the Reformation emphasized in life. We must now add a third: suffering. And again we use the word in its broadest significance, not merely the visible suffering that comes through illness, misfortune, or the death of persons we love. This is only the severest, most concentrated form of suffering. Nobody escapes it and we must constantly be prepared to meet it. But it is all the more important to know that all of life rests upon an unseen foundation of suffering, deprivation, and sacrifice. We all live by reason of the fact that men perform hard physical labor for us or that others bear political responsibility for us. When war comes, a part of the nation, to our eyes chosen at haphazard, are compelled to make the supreme sacrifice and others are spared. Without this law of vicarious sacrifice and suffering there would be no life. We do not really live our life to the full until we are willing to take upon ourselves that part of it that falls to us.

115

These three dimensions, loving, working, and suffering, describe the whole of life. Everything that happens to us has its place in it. God wants the whole of our life. But when we look at these dimensions we begin to understand that we cannot live this life by our own strength, but only by grace. And this is the heart of the Reformation message. It is the strong comfort in our failure and our hope that, if we have God with us on our way, we shall reach the goal. "This life," said Luther, "is not being devout, but becoming devout, not being whole, but becoming whole . . . not a rest but an exercise. We are not yet, but we shall be. It is not the end, but the way."

IX

The Reformation View of Death

"THIS LIFE IS not being whole, but becoming whole, not a rest, but an exercise. . . . It is not the end, but the way." These words of Luther that sum up the Reformation view of life lead us to the Reformation view of death. Death is the last stretch on the road to health, the door to wholeness. This is a strange juxtaposition to us, but it is the one that the gospel makes: "Death is swallowed up in victory" (I Cor. 15:55). And here we Christians of all churches have been at one, beyond all our differences, from the days of the martyrs of the ancient church, who welcomed the day of their death as the day of their true birth, to the young Munich medical student who before his execution by the Gestapo in 1943 comforted his parents in exactly the same way: "Remember that death does not mean the end of all life, but actually, on the contrary, a birth, a passing over into a new life, a glorious and everlasting life."[18]

Certainly for many this is a thought difficult to accept. A wish-dream, they say. We Christians know that we cannot prove this Christian view of death to anyone. It lies beyond the sphere of the demonstrable, just as does our faith in God or the power of the Holy Spirit over human hearts. We can only beg men to listen to this strange intertwining of death and life which runs so contrary to our shallow-rooted conceptions. Death needs to be seen from the standpoint of life—and life from the standpoint of death.

First, life from the standpoint of death. "The summons of death comes to us all, and no one can die for another. Every one must fight his own battle with death by himself, alone. . . . I will not be with you then, nor you with me." So Luther began the famous series of Lenten sermons he preached in March, 1522, after his hasty return from the Wartburg, the sermons through which he quelled the trouble-makers and iconoclasts in the Wittenberg congregation. "No one can die for another"; each one must die "by himself," in his own person. The loneliness of death is the profoundest expression of the fact that we are persons. In life we can lean on many supports—parents, family traditions, husband or wife, other people who radiate strength, the formulations and instructions of the church. In death, however, man is utterly alone, everything else is left behind. Therefore, as Luther says, a man must be "armed and prepared" for this moment. "I will not be with you then, nor you with me."

Luther said this to the Wittenberg agitators in order to show them the terrible wrong they had done in forcing upon the congregation reforms in worship for which the people were not ready. A faith which is accepted under pressure or in an excess of emotion is worthless, because it will not stand the test in the moment of ultimate loneliness. Luther based the love and patience (today we would say, the tolerance) which we owe to one another in questions of faith upon ultimate, solitary responsibility of man before God in which no one else in this world can help him. From the viewpoint of death it is clear that any coercion of people in matters of faith, and also, for example, any prevention of worship, is the deepest kind of violation of human personality. In the struggle for religious truth the only weapon that can be used is the convincing Word of God.

But this view of death in solitude determines not only our relation to one another but also our own life. None of us lives on probation. Everything we do is irrevocable. True, we can try to make amends for some mistake, as we say all too sanguinely, but we cannot undo anything that has been done. True, we can recall to memory an experience of great happiness, but we cannot repeat it. Death not only stands at the end of our life; it walks beside us from our very birth. Our time trickles minute by minute into its hand until the measure is full. At first we do not notice this and hardly even think about it. But the mysterious mixture of gaining things and then leaving them all behind, of triumphs and then extinction, which constitutes our life, can sweep down upon us and oppress us in youth, but it does so even more the older we grow. It is a good thing not to evade this but rather to be aware of this irrevocability in everything we do. It is not death that is our last hour; rightly understood, all our hours are last hours. We can use them or let them slip away, we can enjoy the beauty of them or fritter it away, we can act and speak energetically and responsibly or carelessly allow our life to pass away, gray, colorless, and only half lived. It is not so that thinking about death need make our life darker. On the contrary, life can become brighter and richer, the colors can become more beautiful, when we know that we do not have unlimited time. "Oh, love while you can still love." "We must work . . . while it is day" (John 9:4).

Of course, to be able to think of the resistless, terribly swift passing of our existence in this way means that we cannot keep making claims upon life and cannot be constantly counting up what it still owes us. Reflection upon death will preserve us from doing this. For it reminds us of the claims God makes of us in our life and what we still owe. A man must be made of cement if the thought of the final reckoning upon his life does not prick his conscience. It is well to think about it before it is too late. It helps us to love, to make the most of the time, to hear the commands of God better. It is only death that makes our life fully earnest and thus also full of life and full of deep joy. The word for the life of a man one day will not be, *Les jeux sont faits,* the game is over. For our life is not a game; it is human life and that means personal, spiritual, responsible life. We are not children and not animals.

We really see life only as we look at it from the viewpoint of death—and we see death only from the viewpoint of life. The man who learns to see his life in view of the end, when the appalling deficiencies in the account will be exposed and can no longer be covered up, will no longer rely upon his good will, his respectable character, and the work he performs in life to gain esteem. One can make an impression in life with this kind of thing only for a certain time, and then only upon the uninitiated. But how about God, who knows all things? And how about ourselves, when we can no longer fool ourselves into thinking that we will change in the future? Then there will be no future.

The incredibly wonderful thing about the gospel is that it says to us: Nevertheless, there is a future. But this is by no means a self-evident and automatic thing. There is nothing in ourselves that has any future at all. It would also be a delusion to believe that at death our immortal soul will separate from the body and enter the realm of the spirit. Man cannot be that easily divided. As we are capable of seeing and thinking of him, he is a totality; the soul is not dependent on the body, the body is not dependent on the soul. From a purely human, philosophical point of view we cannot get beyond the conclusion that death is final. Only from the outside, from outside ourselves, can any certainty be given to us; only if we know God to be the sustaining reality of our life. The reality—not merely a philosophical idea that obtrudes itself or forces itself upon us, but rather the constant, living vis-à-vis of our life. We live by him, we live beneath his eye, we live with him as our goal. Only as we sense his hand above us, leading and providing for us in life, can we be certain that his eternal hand will never let us go. We do not become immortal through our spiritual or moral acts; we can only let ourselves be drawn by God into his life. Eternal life means nothing else but to be with God. We must let go of all the other ideas we have conceived about it. We know absolutely nothing. But just as absolutely we can believe that God's search for our hearts here in this life is an invitation to his eternal life. We shall not grow up into eternal life simply of ourselves when we leave our earthly body. Rather God will complete the work that he begins in us here.

To let God begin his work—this is what faith means. The way to eternal life begins only with a wholly personal faith in God who knows me and calls me. In the face of this utter and radical end which is death, it takes a tremendous courage to believe in our everlasting life. Wish-dreams will not be enough here, but only the certainty that it is promised and assured to us by him who is the Lord of our life and all of life, before whose majesty we bow. And that is pure grace. With what could we possibly earn everlasting life? Nor is it a matter of God doing half and we doing the other half; it is only God's mighty hand that takes us out of death into his life.

So the words "by grace alone," the message of the gospel and the Reformation, are proclaimed in the face of death and eternity. In this faith death becomes the door to life, the step to that full and final health and wholeness in which sin and incompleteness no longer distort our being.

God is nearer to me than I am to myself. This is what we said in connection with a thought suggested by Luther in our discussion of the Reformation view of God. In the face of death this truth reveals itself to the full.

Notes

1. Vatican Council (1870), *Sessio* I, *Cap.* 2. Antimodernist oath (1910).

2. *Weimar Ausgabe* (WA) 10 I 2, 168, 22 ff.

3. This reference is unfortunately obscured in the English translation of the *Heidelberg Disputation, Luther's Works,* Vol. 31 (Philadelphia, Muhlenberg Press, 1957), p. 52, where in Thesis 20 the words *"posteriora Dei"* are translated "the manifest things of God," thus losing Luther's allusion to the passage in Deuteronomy. (Trans.)

4. *WA* 34 I, 132, 8, 20, 27; 108, 24.

5. *WA* 10 I 1; 44, 18. (The reference to the "little, near face" alludes to the face of the infant Jesus, the context being Luther's Christmas postil on Titus 2:11–15. Trans.)

6. *WA* 7, 721, 32.

7. *WA* 7, 586, 15.

8. *WA* 10 II, 182, 34.

9. *WA* 8, 412, 1.

10. *WA* 1, 557, 33.

11. *WA* 8, 412, 14; 483, 16.

12. *WA* 2, 449, 5.

13. *WA* 8, 412, 4.

14. *WA* 2, 586, 15 ff.

15. Karl Adam in *Theologische Quartalschrift* 130, 1950, p. 282.

16. Sessio IV.

17. Carl Feckes, *Zur kommenden Definierung der Himmelfahrt Mariens* (Leutesdorf a. Rh., Johannes-Verlag, 1950), p. 3.

18. Alexander Schmorell in the collection of "final messages and records of the Resistance" edited by Helmut Gollwitzer, Käthe Kuhn, and Reinhold Schneider, *Dying We Live*, tr. by Reinhard C. Kuhn (New York: Pantheon Books Inc., 1956), p. 56.

Index

Adam, Karl, 93
Assumption of Mary, 92, 93, 94
Augustine, 49, 67

Bach, Johann Sebastian, 23 ff.
Baptism, 40
Beethoven, Ludwig van, 30, 103
Bodelschwingh, Friedrich von, 80
Brenz, John, 47
Bruno, Giordano, 101
Bucer, Martin, 47
Buddha, 29, 31

Cajetan, Cardinal, 87
Calvin, John, 67
Charles V, Emperor, 91
Church, 52 f., 57 ff., 75 ff., 85 f.

Confucius, 29
Conscience, 26, 70, 107
Council of Basil, 83
Council of Trent, 90, 93

Death, 117 ff.
Dignity, human, 25, 26, 27

Enlightenment, the, 17
Erasmus, Desiderius, 27, 28

Faith, 15 ff., 52, 69, 75, 104, 121
Francis of Assisi, 67
Freedom, 27, 70, 71

Gandhi, Mahatma, 80
George, Duke of Saxony, 84

125

Index

Goethe, J. W., 29, 30, 32, 33, 101
Good works, 16, 22, 27, 51, 75

History, 72 f.
Holy Spirit, 60, 61, 62, 64, 77, 93, 118

Immaculate Conception of Mary, 92
Infallibility, papal, 92

Justification, 20, 51, 71

Kant, Immanuel, 19, 51
Kingdom of God, 65, 66, 68, 70, 71, 72, 73, 75

Lavater, Johann Kasper, 30
Leo X, Pope, 91
Lord's Supper, 40
Lortz, Joseph, 90
Love, 22, 52, 75, 79 f., 107, 113
Luther, Martin, 20, 22, 23, 27, 28, 29, 41, 57 ff., 66 ff., *passim*
   "theology of the cross," 23, 45 ff.
   Heidelberg Disputation, 46 ff., 51, 53
   Ninety-five Theses, 46, 53, 80
   Large Catechism, 57, 58
   Treatise on Good Works, 75

Man, 74, 105 ff.
Marx, Karl, 32

Merit, 23, 27, 52
Mozart, Wolfgang Amadeus, 32

Napoleon, 67
Neighbor, 29, 32, 75
Nietzsche, Friedrich, 32

Paul, Apostle, 23, 31, 33, 40
Pierre, Abbé, 80
Pius IX, Pope, 94
Pius XII, Pope, 83
Plato, 29, 31, 32

Reason, 107 f.
Repentance, 80

Sanctification, 59 ff.
Schiller, J. C. F., 103
Schweitzer, Albert, 36, 80
Scriptures, 36 ff., 86, 90, 91, 93, 94
Socrates, 30, 31
Suffering, 115
Sunday observance, 57 ff.

"theology of glory," 47 f.
Thomist theology, 51
Time, 72 f.

Vatican Council, First, 94
Vocation, 113 ff.

Word of God, 35, 54, 58, 59, 62, 77

A